101
Nature
Experiments

101
Nature
Experiments

Written by
DAVID BURNIE

DORLING KINDERSLEY
London • New York • Stuttgart

A DORLING KINDERSLEY BOOK

Editor Helena Spiteri
Designers Susan St Louis, Ivan Finnegan
Managing editor Gillian Denton
Managing art editor Julia Harris
Assistant editor Susila Baybars
Production Catherine Semark
Special photography
Andy Crawford, Steve Gorton

First published in Great Britain in 1996
by Dorling Kindersley Limited,
9 Henrietta Street, London WC2E 8PS

4 6 8 10 9 7 5 3

A CIP catalogue record for this book is
available from the British Library

ISBN 0 7513 5381 7

Colour reproduction by Colourscan, Singapore
Printed and bound in China by L.Rex Printing Co., Ltd.

Be a safe naturalist
• **Always** follow the steps in each experiment carefully.
• **Take care** especially when handling hot or heavy objects.
• **Make sure** you clean up after each experiment.

This sign means that extra care is needed.
Ask an adult to help you.

This sign means that you should never disturb an
animal in its home or take it away from its natural habitat.

Contents

THE WORLD AROUND US

LIFE IN WATER

LIFE IN SOIL

PLANTS AND GROWTH

THE WORLD AROUND US

THE WORLD IS FULL of many kinds of living things. Some move around, others spend their lives rooted in one place. A few are taller than a house, and some are so tiny they can only be seen with a microscope. Despite all these differences, living things do have some features in common. They all need oxygen and water to survive, and they are all made up of tiny units called cells.

1 Is air really there?

Air is all around us. When it moves, it presses against everything in its path. But unless it is blowing about, we seldom feel that it is actually there. In this experiment you will see air at work. By sealing a funnel to a glass jar, you will see what happens when water tries to get in without air being able to get out.

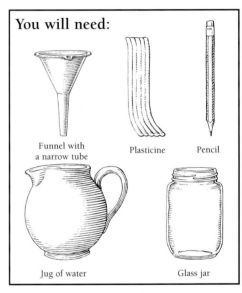

You will need:

Funnel with a narrow tube

Plasticine

Pencil

Jug of water

Glass jar

1. Put the funnel in the mouth of the jar and mould a layer of plasticine around the join.

2. Make sure that you have enough plasticine to circle the jar. Press a piece of plasticine firmly to seal it against the funnel and the jar. When you have done this, look carefully to make sure there are no gaps where air could escape.

3. Slowly pour some water into the funnel. If the funnel is narrow enough you may find that a little water trickles through, but the water will soon stop. The rest of the water stays in the funnel, even though its end is open.

If you colour the water you will see it more clearly

Air pushes on the water in the funnel and holds it there

Hole made by pencil

4. The water cannot get into the jar because the jar is already full of air that cannot get out.

5. Carefully make a hole through the plasticine with a pencil. Slowly remove the pencil, and watch what happens next.

6. The air can now escape from the jar. As soon as this happens, the water pours into the jar, taking up the space the air once filled.

3 See a plant drink

Plants suck up water through tiny pipelines in their roots and stems, and let it evaporate (turn into a vapour) through microscopic holes in their leaves and flowers. Water helps a plant grow and keep its cells firm, so it does not wilt. In this experiment, you will see how water moves up a stem, into a flower. A brightly coloured dye shows where the water goes.

👬 *Adult supervision is advised*

Water has travelled up the stem to the petals

You will need:

Sticky tape

Food colouring
PLUS Pale-coloured flower

2 glasses

Sharp knife

1. Fill glasses with water. Add some food colouring to one of them, and stir well.
2. Lay the flower on a work surface and carefully slice its stem in two. Work from the bottom of the stem, stopping halfway up.
3. Wind some tape around the end of the cut to prevent the stem from splitting further.
4. Put each stem half into a glass. Lean the flower against a wall or window.
5. In an hour, the food colouring should begin to colour half of the flower.

Tape prevents stem from splitting

2 Test your breath

When you breathe, your body gives up water to the air outside. The water you breathe out forms an invisible vapour. When your warm breath hits a cold mirror you will see it turn back into a liquid.

You will need:

Hand mirror

Put the mirror in the fridge for an hour. Wipe it, hold it close to your mouth, and breathe on it. Water vapour in your breath turns into drops of water, making the mirror turn misty. The colder the mirror the more easily drops form.

4 Measure water loss through a leaf

Every day a tree sucks up water from the soil and lets it evaporate from its leaves. But how much water vapour actually escapes from a single leaf? In this experiment you will measure the amount of water some leaves give off, and divide it by their surface area.

You will need:

Glass jar with volume marks

Jug of water

Squared paper

Crayon

PLUS Cooking oil, Leafy twig

1. Fill a jar with water and add a thin layer of oil. Put the twig in the water, and note the water level. After eight hours check the water level and see how much water has disappeared.

Leaf area is estimated by adding up the squares

2. Use a crayon to draw an outline of each leaf on squared paper and add up the squares inside each outline. Divide the amount of water lost by the number of squares. This shows how much water is lost by each square of the leaf.

The oil seals off the water, making sure it can only escape through the leaves

5 Rot a pepper

In nature nothing is ever wasted. As soon as something dies, it is broken down by other living things, such as moulds and bacteria. This process is called decay, or rotting. Slice open a rip and juicy red pepper or tomato. Leave it for two weeks and see what happens.

Adult supervision is advised

Day one

Day eight

Slice a red pepper in two. Over the next two weeks observe how the mould spreads over the pepper, making it rot.

Day fifteen

6 Natural recycling

Vegetable peelings and leftovers are not very appetizing. But instead of throwing them away, why not put them to good use? If you make a compost heap, you can recycle this kind of waste and turn it into a valuable fertilizer for your garden plants.

Adult supervision is essential

1. Ask an adult to help you make a square box from the boards and posts. Stand the box in a corner of a garden or backyard.

2. Gradually fill the box with the waste you have collected. You can use peelings from the kitchen and weeds from the garden.

3. As the heap builds up, the waste will start to break down. This will happen faster if you keep the heap in a warm and damp place.

4. After several weeks the compost should be ready. You can spread it in a garden to help the plants grow.

You will need:

Screwdriver or Hammer

Screws or nails **PLUS** Posts or brackets, Kitchen and garden waste

Trowel

4 wooden boards, each about 50 cm (20 in) square

Petals

Banana skin

Weeds

Cabbage

Flowers

Vegetable peelings and waste

Decomposed waste makes excellent fertilizer

Mature compost heap

7 Make animal cells

Cells are tiny compartments that make up all living things. Animals have many different cells, and each one has a special job. Some cells enable an animal to move, while others allow it to sense its surroundings. Here you will make a model that resembles a group of animal cells living together.

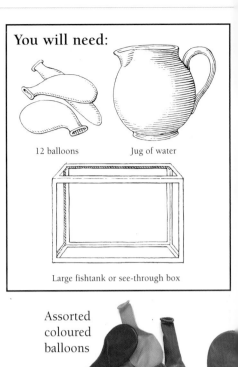
1. Place the tank and balloons on a tabletop. The tank represents a tiny part of an animal's body, the balloons its cells.

Assorted coloured balloons

2. Fit the mouth of each balloon around a cold water tap, and slowly fill them with water. Be careful not to fill the balloons too much.

3. Hold each balloon by the neck. Knot the end to seal the water inside, then slowly place it in the tank.

Real animal cells are surrounded by fluid

5. Pour in enough water to cover the balloons. In a living animal, fluid keeps the cells alive. You now have a model resembling a tiny group of animal cells living together.

4. Keep adding balloons until the tank is full. The balloons must be tightly packed together with only a little space in between.

8 See plant cells

 Adult supervision is advised

Plant cells are not the same as animal cells. Instead of being soft and flexible, they have a tough outer wall that gives them a fixed shape. Some plant cells are much bigger than animal cells, which makes them easier to see. In this experiment you will use a magnifying glass to see cells in an onion.

You will need:

Knife   *PLUS* Onion   Tweezers   Magnifying glass

Onion cells as seen through a microscope at low magnification

1. Cut a small square out of an onion. Using the tweezers, pull away a thin film of onion skin. Press it onto a windowpane so it sticks in position. You should now be able see its cells with the magnifying glass.

In a living animal, fluid keeps the cells alive

9 How sugar moves water

Cells must have water to survive. They get water by soaking it up from their surroundings. In this experiment, you will see how raisin cells take in water. The cells in each raisin are dead, but they do contain lots of sugar. The sugar helps to suck in water from outside.

You will need:

Saucer of raisins

Jug of water   Glass jar   Spoon

Raisins

1. Press some raisins between your fingertips. They should feel dry and hard. Now spoon them into a jar.

Swollen raisins

2. Add enough water so that you almost fill the jar. Even though the raisins are now underwater, they still look very dry and shrivelled.

3. Give the raisins a good stir, and leave them in the jar. The sugar in the raisin cells will slowly draw in some of the water.

4. After three hours, look at the jar again. The cells have taken in so much water that the raisins are now swollen and plump.

10 Living together

Where can you find the biggest variety of plants and animals? Which things often live side by side? Find out the answers to these questions by using a wooden square called a quadrat. A quadrat is a device that is used to mark out a patch of ground, in order to survey wildlife in different habitats.

Quadrat divides the plants into measured squares

11 How salt moves water

In the experiment opposite, water moves into cells containing sugar. Here, find out what happens when water moves the other direction. This experiment uses potatoes which contain living cells. Salt helps draw water out of the cells.

You will need:

Jug of water   Knife   Spoon   Saucer   2 bowls   Chopping board

PLUS Salt, Potatoes

1. Cut the potatoes into large pieces and remove the skin. Notice how hard the potato feels.

Cubed potatoes

2. Fill the two bowls with water. Add some salt to one bowl, but leave the other as it is.

3. Stir the salt to help it dissolve. Don't worry if some is left at the bottom of the bowl.

4. Add some pieces of potato to each bowl. Leave them for about two hours. Then pick them up and compare them.

5. The cells in salty surroundings have lost water, making the potato feel soft and rubbery. The cells in pure water are unchanged.

1. Assemble and screw the pieces of wood together to make a square frame. Using a ruler and pencil, divide each side into quarters. Stretch the string across the quarter marks, and fasten with the drawing pins. The frame is now divided into 16 squares.

2. Put the frame on the ground, and record the plants and animals in each small square on some squared paper.

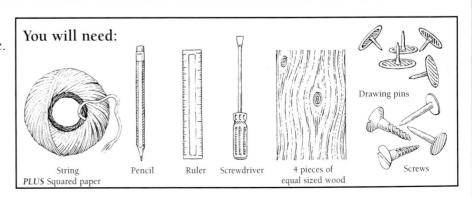

You will need:

String   Pencil   Ruler   Screwdriver   4 pieces of equal sized wood   Drawing pins   Screws

PLUS Squared paper

LIFE IN WATER

ALL PLANTS AND ANIMALS need water to survive. About three-quarters of our planet is covered with water. Most of it is salty, and makes up the seas and oceans. Freshwater comes from rain, and flows in streams and rivers. Unlike seawater, it contains little or no salt. Freshwater only includes a fraction of the water on our planet, but it is an important habitat for wildlife.

12 Filter water

When it rains, some water goes into streams and rivers, the rest sinks into the ground. As rain moves through holes in rock and soil, it gets filtered, and by the end of its journey it is clean. In this experiment you will see how this filtering process works.

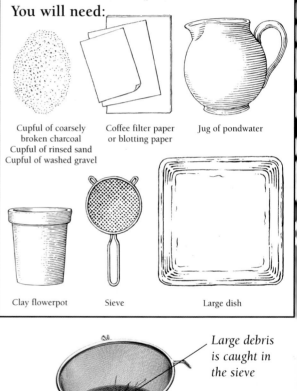

You will need:

Cupful of coarsely broken charcoal
Cupful of rinsed sand
Cupful of washed gravel

Coffee filter paper or blotting paper

Jug of pondwater

Clay flowerpot

Sieve

Large dish

1. Line a flowerpot with filter paper. Fill a third of it with charcoal. Rinse some sand in a sieve and pack it onto the charcoal. Fill the rest of the flowerpot with gravel.

2. Collect some pondwater in a jug. Hold the sieve over the flowerpot, and gently pour the dirty pondwater in a steady steam through it.

The sand inside traps small pieces of dirt

The charcoal and filter paper traps tiny particles of dirt

Large debris is caught in the sieve

Filtered water collects in the dish

3. Wait until all the dirty pondwater has passed through the the layers of charcoal, sand, and gravel. Now remove the flowerpot from the tray, and pour the clean water back into the jug. The water is now much cleaner. But do not drink it!

13 Train fish with sound

Fish can hear sounds from outside a fish tank. If you have some goldfish, you can carry out this simple experiment in animal behaviour, and see how fish will learn to associate sound with food.

You will need:

Bell
PLUS Fish

Fish tank

Set up a regular routine of ringing a bell just before you feed the fish. If you do this for several days, you will find that the fish learn the sound of the bell means food. As soon as they hear it, they will expect to eat.

14 Make an aquarium

A freshwater aquarium is like an indoor pond. Fill it with plants and animals that normally live together, and you can see how they feed and grow. Put the tank somewhere bright, but keep it away from direct sunlight so the water does not get too warm.

You will need:

Fish tank

Trowel

Jug of water

Aquarium gravel and rocks

PLUS Water plants and animals

1. Rinse the gravel, and then spread it out in a layer on the base of the tank. Next, add rocks, so the animals have somewhere to hide, and a surface on which to feed.

2. Add enough water to half-fill the tank. Use rainwater – or better still, use water from a pond. Add rooted plants in their pots, or plant them in the gravel. Add pond weed directly into the water.

Leaves provide oxygen

Snails

Plants in the tank provide food for the animals

3. Your aquarium is now ready to receive its animal inhabitants. If you have filled the tank with pond water, you may find that it already contains tiny floating animals, such as water fleas. If you add some pond snails, they will scrape tiny plants off the rocks and glass, and help keep the tank clean. If you decide to add some fish, remember to feed them, or they will soon eat all the tank's smaller inhabitants.

15 Going green

In nature, pure water is hard to find. It nearly always contains dissolved chemicals and tiny organisms. The water we drink is different, as most of these things have been removed. In this experiment you will compare three types of water, to see how many microscopic plants they contain.

You will need:

3 glass jars

Pond water, filtered water, and tap water *PLUS* Liquid plant fertilizer

1. Fill each glass jar with a different kind of water. Add a single drop of plant fertilizer to each one to encourage plant growth.

2. Leave the jars on a sunny windowsill for a few days. In the sunshine, the invisible water plants will slowly start to multiply.

Pond water turns green when plant fertilizer is added

3. Look at the jars. Compare the colour of the water in each one. The water that contained tiny plants will slowly turn green. The water that had few or no plants will stay clear for much longer.

16 Walking on water

Did you know that water has a "skin"? Some small insects, called pondskaters, are so light that they can walk across this skin without sinking. If you have steady hands, you can see the skin for yourself in this quick and easy experiment.

You will need:

Small bowl   Tweezers   Needle   Jug of water

1. Fill the bowl with water, and wait for a minute until the surface is completely still.

2. Pick up the needle with the tweezers. Hold the needle horizontally so that it is level with the water's surface. Lower it slowly until it touches the water.

3. When the needle meets the water, open the tweezers. The needle should sit on the water's surface. If you break the water's skin, the needle will sink.

17 Trap underwater animals

In ponds, small animals often feed at night, when darkness hides them from their enemies. But strangely, the same animals are often attracted to light. In this experiment you can use light to lure some of these animals into a trap, so that you can examine them more closely.

1. Tape the funnel to one end of the pipe, with the narrow end pointing into the tube. Switch on the torch, and put it into the jar. Screw the lid on to stop water from coming in.

2. Put the jar in the pipe with the light shining through the funnel. Fasten the plastic over the open end of the pipe with the elastic bands.

3. Tie the string around both ends of the pipe, leaving it slack in the middle to make a handle. Lower it into the pond carefully and leave it there overnight.

You will need:

Waterproof sticky tape

Small torch

Elastic bands

Funnel

Glass jar with lid

Black plastic

String

Wide plastic pipe

PLUS Bucket (optional)

4. In the morning, pull up the trap, remove the black plastic, and pour the water inside it into a bucket or bowl. Now examine what you have caught. Put the animals back in the pond when you have finished.

Small animals swim in through the wide spout of the funnel, but cannot find their way out

18 Make a rockpool viewer

Coastal rockpools are like tiny worlds teeming with life. Each one has plants and animals that live there permanently, cut off by the tide. These species must adapt to the varying conditions, as the pool often heats up when the tide is out, and then cools down as fresh water spills in. With the help of this device, you can get a clear view of the inhabitants of a rockpool.

Adult supervison is advised

You will need:

Waterproof sticky tape

Felt-tip pen

Plastic pipe 30 cm (1 ft) long

PLUS Sheet of perspex, Saw

Put one end of the pipe on the perspex, and draw around it with the pen. Ask an adult to cut out the circle with a saw. Tape this to one end of the pipe, making sure that there are no gaps where water might be able to get in.

With your viewer you might see sea anemones and starfish like these

19 Make a beachcomber's showcase

There is always plenty to do at the seaside. You can paddle in the sea, explore the shore in search of plants and seashore wildlife, and collect plenty of colourful shells and pebbles. Here you will find out how to make an attractive showcase to display the shells that you find.

You will need:

Sticky tape   Pencil   Labels

Scissors   Card   Ruler

PLUS Collection of shells

1. With the help of a ruler, cut out 16 strips of card that are 2.5 cm (1 in) in width.

Collection of shells

Lines are produced as the shell grows

2. Take a fresh sheet of card, and draw a rectangle as long as the strips. Add a margin of 2.5 cm (1 in) around it, and then cut it out.

3. Fold up the margin around the rectangle to make four sides. Fasten them upright with some sticky tape.

4. Use the strips of card to partition the case into small sections. You will need to cut slots in the strips to make them fit together.

5. Stick each strip to the edge of the showcase. Now you are ready to fill the showcase with your favourite shells.

6. Label each of your shells. Write down what kind it is, and the date and place you found it.

🌿 *Protect the natural world*

Clever collector

Only collect empty shells that are washed up on the beach. Don't be tempted to collect shells that still contain living animals, because they will soon die.

All sorts of shells

Apart from at the seaside, you can find different kinds of empty shells in woods, parks, and beside the edges of ponds or streams. You might even find some in a garden.

Some shells are fragile, so handle them with care

20 See inside a shell

Shells are portable homes made by animals such as cockles and snails. Some shells are shaped like saucers, but others are wound up in a tight spiral, making it very difficult to look inside. If you use some sandpaper, you can scrape holes in shells, and see how they are built.

Collection of shells

1. Cut a piece of sandpaper. Hold the shell against the sandpaper, and rub it backwards and forwards. Be sure to keep your fingers out of the way.

2. After a while, the sandpaper will rub right through the shell. You will soon see a spiral chamber where the shell's inhabitant lived.

19

21 Make a mini-pond

Making a pond is a great way of attracting water wildlife into your garden. A big pond can be home to many different plants and animals, but if you don't have much room a mini-pond is almost as good. Here, you can find out how to make a mini-pond from a bucket or shallow bowl. If you add some water plants to your mini-pond you should attract some small water animals.

You will need:

Jug of water   Trowel   Bucket or shallow bowl

PLUS Assorted flowering plants, Water plants, Assorted shells, Rocks or beach boulders

Pondweed

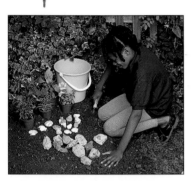

1. Find an open and sunny spot in the garden in which to place the pond. Dig a hole that is as deep as the bucket.

2. Lower the empty bucket into the hole, making sure that it fits snugly. The rim should be level with the soil.

3. Firm the loose soil around the bucket, so there are no gaps. Now you are ready to decorate it to make it look more natural.

4. Take the plants out of their pots and plant them around the edge of the pond. Add a few shells and pebbles in between.

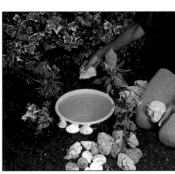

5. Fill the pond with water. You can use tapwater but it is better to use rainwater if you can collect enough. Add some rocks to the pond so that the water animals have somewhere to hide. Build them up until they reach the rim to enable any small wild animals that fall in a way out. Now add some water plants.

Life in the pond

The plants will help to supply oxygen to the water. As the weeks go by they will attract small animals, such as damselflies. They fly to ponds, and lay their eggs in the water. Many insects start their life in the water and take to the air when they become adults.

22 Test water for acidity

Plants and animals that live in water are easily harmed when pollution in the air makes the water acidic. This happens when poisonous gases from cars or factories spread through the air. When rainwater falls through the gases it becomes acidic. In this experiment you will make your own acid water with a little vinegar, and then use some strips of litmus paper to test it. When water contains acid, the litmus paper immediately changes colour. Continue the experiment by testing rainwater and the water from a pond, to see if they are acidic.

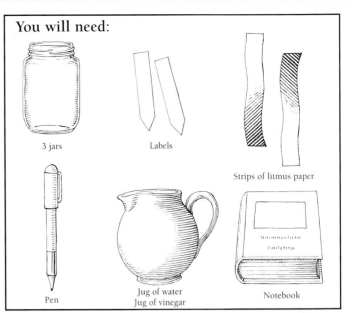

You will need:

3 jars
Labels
Strips of litmus paper
Pen
Jug of water
Jug of vinegar
Notebook

1. Fill the first jar with tapwater and label it. Pour enough water into the second jar to make it three-quarters full, and top it up with vinegar. Label it "Slightly acid."

2. Fill the third jar with an equal amount of water and vinegar. This mixture is more concentrated than the one in the second jar, so label it "Stronger acid."

3. Now dip the litmus paper into each jar and write down the results in your notebook. The litmus paper turns pink when it soaks up water containing vinegar (regardless of how much vinegar is in the water). The litmus paper darkens slightly in tapwater because it is wet.

Strips of litmus paper

Litmus paper darkens slightly

Jar of water

Litmus paper turns pink in slightly acid water

"Slightly acid"

"Stronger acid"

Litmus paper turns pink in stronger acidic water

21

LIFE IN SOIL

IN THE SOIL BENEATH our feet is a hidden world of living things. Some of them creep or scuttle among the fallen leaves. Others dig burrows, or eat their way through the ground. You can find out about the living world in the soil, and with the help of some simple equipment meet some of its tiny inhabitants.

23 Test the soil

The quality and appearance of soil varies a great deal. In some places is deep and rich, while in others, it is thin, dry, and dusty. Life in the soil also varies. For example, very few animals can survive in wet, acidic soil. But alkaline soil is rich in minerals and supports an abundance of animal life. In this experiment you will use red and blue litmus paper to test soil and see whether it is acidic or alkaline.

You will need:

Soil

Spoon

Red litmus paper
Blue litmus paper

Distilled water

Jar with lid

1. Collect a small sample of soil, and put a spoonful of it in a jar. Use the spoon to break up any big lumps.

Soil sample

2. Half-fill the jar with distilled water. This will dissolve the chemicals in the prepared soil. Now screw on the lid of the jar, making sure that it is tight.

3. Shake the jar quite hard, for at least one minute, to mix the soil and water well. Leave the jar to stand on a flat surface until the soil has completely settled.

4. Place two strips of litmus paper on the tabletop. Unscrew the jar, and dip the handle of the spoon into the mixture.

5. Dab the handle onto each of the paper strips, so that each one is wetted. See which one of the litmus papers changes colour.

Blue litmus paper turns red

Red litmus paper turns blue

6. If the soil is acid, the red litmus paper turns blue. If the soil is alkaline, the blue litmus paper turns red.

24 Keeping cool

On a warm, sunny day, the surface of the soil soon heats up and gets too hot and dry for some soil animals. Beneath the surface, it is very different. Use a thermometer, and you will see that even when the surface of the soil is warm the soil below the surface always remains cool.

1. Leave one thermometer aside to measure the temperature of the air. Find a sunny patch in the garden (or somewhere outside), and dig a small hole.

2. Push one thermometer in the surface of the soil. This will tell you the temperature of the top layer of soil.

3. Now put the third thermometer into the hole you have dug. Then fill it with soil so that only the top of the thermometer is showing. Leave it for ten to fifteen minutes.

Air is cooler than the surface of soil

Hottest place is the surface of the soil

Beneath the surface of the soil it is even cooler than the air

4. Now remove the thermometer and read it. You should find that the temperature beneath the surface of the soil is cooler than the temperature of the air, and much cooler than the temperature of the surface of the soil higher up. The coolness of the soil keeps small animals comfortable and stops them from getting too hot and drying out.

25 Make a pit trap

During the night, when we are asleep, many small animals are wide awake. They wander far and wide looking for food, but they move silently, and leave few signs that they have passed by. By the time we wake up, they have already hidden themselves away. If you want to see these animals, you don't have to stay up all night. Instead, you can make the simple pit trap shown here. It holds small animals without harming them, and lets you look at them during the day.

You will need:

Pencil

Trowel

Small bowl

Saucer

Notebook

Glass jar

Piece of wood or tile

PLUS 4 stones, Food for bait

A piece of wood

Four large stones

A cube of cheese

Biscuit crumbs

A piece of apple

A piece of meat

1. Dig a hole in the ground large enough to hold the glass jar. Pack the loose soil around the jar to hold it in place. Make sure that the rim is level with the ground's surface, so the animals fall in easily.

2. Put some bait in the jar. You can use the bait shown here, but any small scraps of leftover food will do, particularly those with strong smells. The smell of the bait will attract passing animals.

3. Put the large stones around the four corners of the trap, and place the wood or tile on top. This will prevent rain from getting into the trap and harming any animals that have been caught.

4. In the morning, take the lid off the trap, lift out the jar and empty your catch into a bowl. When you have examined them, put the creatures back.

5. Now try varying the bait to see if different kinds of food attract different animals. Try fruit and biscuit crumbs one night, and then meat the next.

6. Set up several traps in different places to see if the type of visitors vary. Record your results in a notebook, to show where different creatures live.

Supporting stones

The cover stops big animals from eating the food

Check trap during the day to see if day visitors differ from night visitors

Small creatures cannot climb up the steep sides

The smell of cheese attracts different animals

25

26 Look at life in the soil

The surface layers of the soil are full of small creatures. Many of them feed on the remains of dead plants. Others are tiny hunters that search for their prey in the soil. Most soil animals hide away from light, which makes them hard to see. Here, you will use light to make them come into the open.

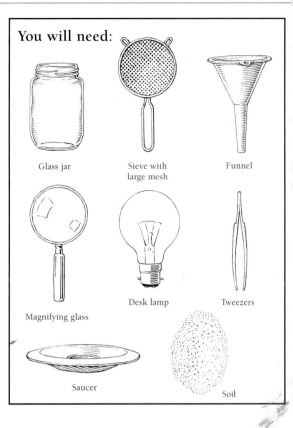

You will need:

Glass jar Sieve with large mesh Funnel

Magnifying glass Desk lamp Tweezers

Saucer Soil

Angled lamp is ideal for flexibility

Make sure the sieve is firmly positioned in the funnel

1. Place the funnel in the glass jar. Add a small amount of soil to the sieve, and rest the sieve in the funnel. Bring the lamp close to the soil, and switch it on. Leave the lamp shining on the soil for about half an hour. The light and warmth will drive tiny soil animals downwards into the jar.

The animals emerge through the spout of the funnel

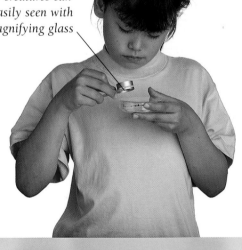

Tiny creatures can be easily seen with a magnifying glass

2. Tip the animals into the saucer, separate them with the tweezers, and examine them using the magnifying glass. You will achieve different results if you use soil from different places, like a woodland or a vegetable patch.

27 Make a worm farm

Earthworms are among the most important animals in the soil. As they eat their way through the soil, they help mix it up, improving its fertility. They bring minerals up from the bottom layers and take dead plant matter down from the top. Make a worm farm in a jar and you can see all this activity.

You will need:

Soil, Sand

Bowl

Water spray
PLUS Leaves, Earthworms

Glass jar

Trowel

1. Spray the soil and sand to make them moist. Build up separate layers until the jar is full. It is essential that the earthworms have plenty of moisture, so keep the layers damp.

2. Add the worms to the jar with care. Five or six worms should be enough to occupy a large glass jar.

3. Cover the worms with the leaves. Put the farm in a cool, dark place. Every few days check the jar for activity.

Earthworms

Dead leaves

Sand

Soil

Leaves dragged down into soil

Soil

Layers of sand and soil emerge from the activity of the earthworms

Active worm farm

Worm tunnels

Leaves

28 Running for cover

Most soil animals spend their lives hidden away, either under leaves, or in the earth. This helps to protect them from their enemies and stops their bodies from drying out. It also makes it difficult for us to see them. In this experiment, you can see how soil animals react when their underground world suddenly changes. Some of them stay where they are, but others look for a safer hideout.

1. Put the square of cloth on the ground. Use the trowel to dig up a mixture of earth and weeds. Put this in the centre of the cloth, spreading it out to form a thin layer.

2. Now watch to see what happens. You will probably see some animals moving across the cloth as they head for shelter. Spiders and centipedes usually act quickly, while slugs and snails react more slowly.

Keeping damp
We have thick skin, which keeps moisture in our bodies. But many soil animals have thin skin, so they depend on moisture in the soil to survive. If they are exposed, they can easily dry out and die.

Snail

Ladybird

29 What substances are in soil?

Imagine trying to make some soil. You would need lots of different ingredients – but what are they, and where would you get them? This experiment will help you find out. Soil is made of two main substances: minerals and organic matter. Minerals come from rocks and are found in the form of tiny stones or specks of grit that sink in water. The rest of soil is made up of humus, or organic matter, which often floats. Humus comes from the remains of plants and animals. When a soil sample is mixed with water it will separate into these substances, forming different layers, according to their weight and size.

You will need:

Jug of water

Glass jars with lids

Soil samples

Mixture of earth and grass

Put the cloth near earth that is covered by leaves

1. Collect small quantities of soil from different places, such as in the woods or garden. Put a small sample of each in the glass jars.

2. Add enough water to each jar to sufficiently cover the soil – about double its volume. Screw the lids on tightly. Mark each jar so you know where the soil comes from.

3. Shake each jar hard for about half a minute. This will separate the different substances in the soil so that they float or sink.

4. Leave the jars to stand for a few minutes. Most of the mineral particles will sink, while the organic matter will float. You will be able to see which kind of soil has the most organic matter.

PLANTS AND GROWTH

PLANTS ARE ABLE to live and grow on sunlight, water, and air. Light gives plants the energy they need. Air and water, together with chemicals from the soil, make up their building materials. In warm and wet places, some plants grow over 90 m (300 ft) tall! In cold places, others can take years to grow a tiny amount.

30 Detect the growing point

Grass is one of nature's most important plants. But have you ever wondered how it survives being eaten, or cut by a lawnmower? Compare growing cress and grass seedlings to find out.

You will need:

2 planting trays

Scissors

Soil or potting compost

Grass and cress seeds

1. Fill both trays with the soil, and sow each with different seeds. When the seedlings are 5 cm (2 in) high, cut them at the base.

2. Watch what happens to the different plants. After a week, your cress seedlings will not have grown back.

3. This box contains grass seedlings that are ready to be cut. They have quickly taken root and formed a dense mat of long, narrow leaves.

4. A week after you cut them, your grass seedlings will look like this. Instead of coming to a halt, they continue to grow. Grass plants can do this because they grow from a point very close to the ground. If their leaves are cut off, they grow up again. Cress grows from a point at the top of the stem. If it is cut off below this, it is unable to grow back.

31 Watch seeds grow

A bean is a seed which contains a tiny living plant, packed inside a very tough case. A seed also contains a store of food that can keep a plant alive for months, or even years. As long as the seed stays dry, the plant lies dormant, but as soon as it gets thoroughly wet, it starts to grow. Find out what amounts of water and air provide the best conditions for a plant to grow in this experiment.

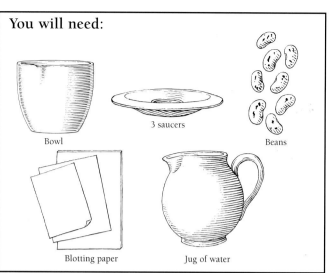

You will need:

Bowl

3 saucers

Beans

Blotting paper

Jug of water

1. Soak the beans in water for 24 hours. This will get them very wet – just as heavy rain would if they were in the ground outside. The beans will be swollen after soaking. Now drain and rinse them.

DAY 5

Beans saturated in water do not have enough air to grow

2. Put a piece of blotting paper on each saucer. Moisten the paper on one of the saucers and keep it damp, but not saturated, during the experiment.

3. Scatter some beans on each of the saucers and spread them out evenly.

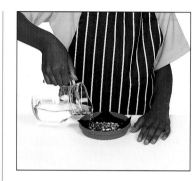

4. Fill one of the saucers containing dry blotting paper with water, so that the beans on it are completely covered and deprived of any air. Leave the last saucer without water.

DAY 5

Only the beans that are left on damp paper germinate and grow

Both water and air are needed for a plant to prosper

32 Grow vegetable tops

Did you know that you can make some vegetables come to life? With the help of water and sunlight, you can watch as their tops begin to sprout new leaves and grow. This experiment works with all root vegetables, which include turnips, radishes, carrots, and parsnips.

Adult supervision is advised

1. Place the turnip on the chopping board. You will only use the top so you can eat what is leftover.

2. Use the knife to cut off the top section of the turnip. The top contains the stem that produces new leaves.

4. Put the saucer on a sunny windowsill. Check the water level every day. As it evaporates, add more water to it.

Watch the stem closely for any change

DAY 1

After a few days the new leaves appear as the turnip comes to life

3. Place the turnip top in a saucer, the cut end face down. Add enough water to it so that it completely covers the cut surface.

DAY 10

DAY 17

The leaves grow bigger, but the vegetable top cannot grow a new root

33 See a bean grow

This experiment lets you see what happens when a broad bean germinates and begins to grow. Normally, the bean would be hidden underground. By growing it in a glass, you can see exactly what happens in its first days of life.

You will need:

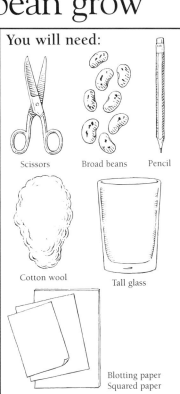

Scissors Broad beans Pencil

Cotton wool Tall glass

Blotting paper
Squared paper

New leaves

Moist cotton wool

Strong roots anchor it in the glass

1. Line the inside of a glass with blotting paper and pack in the cotton wool. Position the bean so it rests between the blotting paper and the glass.

2. Stick a strip of squared paper on the outside close to the bean. Half-fill the glass with water, set aside, and wait for the bean to grow.

3. Use the squared paper to measure how much the bean grows each day. Keep the water level topped up so that the plant does not dry out.

34 Reaching for light

In order to grow, plants need light. They search this out as tirelessly as animals hunt for food. They sense light falling on their stems and react by growing towards it. Plant a climbing bean in a box with a hole in the top and you can watch it as it grows, reaching up towards the light.

You will need:

Sticky tape Scissors

Flowerpot Soil

Matt black paint Climbing beans

Cardboard Paintbrush
PLUS Shoebox

1. Cut a small hole in one end of the box.

2. Cut out two pieces of cardboard as deep as the box, but not quite as wide. Tape them into the box as shown below.

3. Paint the inside of the box black. The black paint will help to absorb any stray light that comes in.

4. Plant the bean in the pot. Water it, and then put it into the box, positioned upright with the hole at the top. Put the lid on the box.

5. Every day, remove the lid to see what is happening inside. Once the bean has germinated, it should find its own way out of the box.

Plant eventually emerges through the hole

35 Freeze leaves

During the winter months, we stay indoors and we wear extra clothing to keep warm. But plants stay outside without protection whatever the weather is like. Some plants have a built-in "antifreeze", to help them survive the cold weather. Others don't, and in very low temperatures, their leaves freeze. When they thaw out they collaspe. See what happens when you freeze two different leaves.

Lettuce leaf

Rhododendron leaves

You will need:

Lettuce leaf
Evergreen leaf such as a Privet, Laurel, or Rhododendron
A freezer

2. As the leaves warm up, any ice crystals will start to melt. See what happens to the leaves when they have completely thawed out.

1. Pick some leaves from an evergreen bush and bring them indoors. Also, cut a leaf from a lettuce. Put both leaves in the freezer and leave them there for about 20 minutes; this will make their temperatures drop to below freezing. Then take the leaves out and lay them on a tabletop.

Thawed lettuce leaf becomes soft and mushy

Surviving the winter
Deciduous plants drop all their leaves in the autumn, and grow a new set in the spring. Evergreen plants have tough leaves that can withstand the winter frost.

Frozen rhododendron leaves

Evergreen leaf keeps its shape

Fair-weather plants
Lettuces are "annual" plants, they do not survive from one year to the next. They die when it gets cold, but their seeds live on, and grow into new plants the following year.

Frozen lettuce leaf

36 Grow a bean upside down

The root of a plant sucks up water and minerals, and also helps to anchor the plant firmly in the soil. Roots grow straight down because they respond to gravity. To see how this happens, grow a bean in a jar. As soon as the root appears, turn it upside down and watch the root change direction.

Glass jar with lid

Bean

Cork

Cotton wool

Glue

Stiff wire

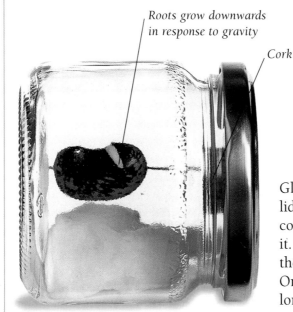

Roots grow downwards in response to gravity

Cork

Glue the cork inside the jar's lid. Push the wire into the cork and thread the bean on it. Put damp cotton wool into the jar, and screw on the lid. Once the root is 1 cm (¹/₂ in) long, rotate the jar 180°.

37 Test a potato for starch

When potato plants grow, they use sunlight to make a substance called starch. It is made in their leaves, but stored underground, in swollen areas called tubers. Starch is a useful substance because it provides us with energy. In this experiment, you can test a potato for starch using a chemical called iodine.

You will need:

Knife

Dropper

Iodine

PLUS Potato

Adult supervision is advised

Slice a potato in half, and then put a few drops of iodine onto the cut side. The iodine will turn from orange-brown to bluish-black. This reaction shows that the potato contains a large amount of starch.

Blue-black iodine

38 Watch sap rise

In your body, blood carries dissolved substances from one place to another. Plants do not have blood, but they do use a liquid to move things about. This liquid is called sap. Normally, sap is hidden away inside a plant, but in this experiment, you can see how sap oozes out when a stem is snapped.

You will need:

Secateurs

Adult supervision is advised

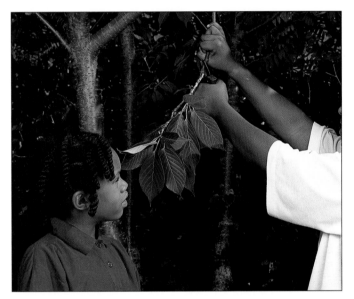

1. Late spring is the best time of year to carry out this experiment. Trees are full of sap because they use the substances it contains to help them grow. Find a tree that has lots of young leafy branches. Carefully cut off one of the branches where it joins the tree. Examine the cut edge, and you should be able to see drops of sap seeping from the wood.

Sticky sap
Special sticky sap oozes out of cuts in the bark of some trees. It works like a liquid sticking plaster, keeping insects and other animals away from the wood while the cut heals.

39 Grow an onion

Although it may look dead, an onion is very much alive. It is waiting for a chance to grow, but it must have water before it can start. In this experiment, you will see what happens if you leave an onion in water.

You will need:

Glass jar

Jug of water

PLUS Onion

1. Fill a glass jar with water. Choose a large onion that feels firm, and rest it in the mouth of the jar.

The bottom of the onion should touch the water

2. After a few weeks, the onion will start to grow roots. These will spread downwards through the water. Some time after the roots have appeared, the onion will start to grow leaves. If you take the onion out of the jar, and place it in the ground, it might flower.

40 Discover root power

Although they are very small, young plants are amazingly strong. Their leaves can lift stones or tarmac as they grow up towards the light, and their roots can fight their way down through the hardest soil in search of water and minerals. The end of a root is covered by a tiny cap that protects it as it grows. In this experiment, you will see how roots are able to break their way out of an eggshell "flowerpot".

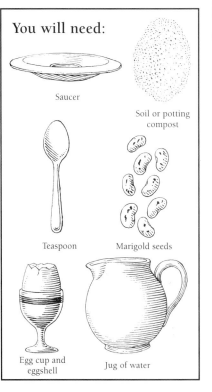

You will need:

Saucer

Soil or potting compost

Teaspoon

Marigold seeds

Egg cup and eggshell

Jug of water

Half-eggshell

1. Using a teaspoon, carefully fill the half-eggshell to the top with some soil.

2. Put the shell in an egg cup and place it on a saucer. Sprinkle the seeds on the top, and cover them with a little soil.

Plant grows from the top of the eggshell

4. Lift up your miniature "flowerpot", and you will see that the roots have forced their way through the shell. Some roots are so strong that they can even push through cracks in rock.

Roots burst through the eggshell

Do not let the soil get soggy

3. Leave in a warm, light place, and water the soil every day. The seeds will germinate and small shoots will appear in a few days.

37

41 Plant fruit pips

Some seeds are as small as specks of dust, but an avocado pit can be as big as a golf ball. If you plant it in a pot, you can grow an avocado plant of your own. Other fruits, such as oranges, apples, grapes, and peaches, contain seeds or pips that you can plant and grow.

You will need:

Flowerpots   Bag ties   Plastic bags   Trowel

Soil or potting compost   Fruit pips and pits   Bowl   Labels

1. Soak the avocado pit in water for 24 hours. Put some soil in a bowl, add some water to make it moist. Stir the soil, and put some into the flowerpots.

2. Plant the avocado pit, pointed end up, so it sticks out of the surface of the soil. The small fruit seeds should be buried, about 1 cm ($\frac{1}{2}$ in) deep into the soil.

3. Label each pot and put it in a plastic bag. Tie up the bags to make sure moisture cannot escape, and then put the pots in a warm, dark place.

Orange pips   Grape seeds

Apple pips

Peach pit

Avocado pit

4. After two to eight weeks, you should start to see signs of life. Take the pots out of the bag, and put them in a place with plenty of light.

Young new leaves

5. Keep the soil well watered, and watch how your fruit trees grow. If roots begin to grow out of the bottom of any pot, it is time to move the plant to a new, bigger one.

The first leaves soon grow large

42 Grow pots of vegetables

Even if you do not have a garden, you can become a vegetable gardener. You can grow vegetables in pots on your windowsill. The best kinds are those that climb, and those that do not spread out too much. Root vegetables often need deep soil, so don't try and grow these unless you have space for very big pots.

You will need:

Labels   Flowerpot or seed tray   Vegetable seeds

Plant sprayer   Trowel   Soil or potting compost

Pen   Bag ties   Garden cane   Plastic bags

1. Fill some pots with soil. If you are growing plants that have small seeds, use a seed tray instead. This will make it easier to separate the seedlings.

2. Plant the seeds, and spray the pots with water. Label, and put them in plastic bags. Keep them in a warm, dark place to help germination.

3. Once the shoots appear, remove the bags and put the pots in the light. Keep them well watered and watch the plants grow.

Young bean forming

Young leaves are a lighter green

New shoot

Garden cane supports a climbing plant

Transfer plant to a bigger pot as it starts to grow

43 Taking cuttings

Plants start life in several different ways. Many grow from seed, but some can also grow from snapped-off stems, or single leaves. By taking cuttings, you can grow new plants without sowing seeds. Here, you can find out how to grow cuttings in soil and in water.

You will need:

Flowerpot

Jug of water

Empty glass

Trowel
PLUS Cuttings

Bowl

Scissors

Soil or potting compost

Growing plantlets

1. The plantlets at the end of a spider plant's runners have roots. When these are 1 cm (½ in) long, cut the plantlet off the runner.

2. Fill the flowerpot with some soil. Push the roots of the plantlet into the soil. Press down the soil around it, so that the cutting is firmly in place.

Taking stem cuttings

1. Cut off a piece of stem about 10 cm (4 in) long, just below the leaf. Trim off the leaves to leave the stem three-quarters bare.

2. So that you can see how a cutting grows roots, put it into a glass of water instead of into soil. Keep the glass full, and once roots appear plant the cutting in soil.

Taking care of your cuttings

Keep your cuttings away from direct sunlight, and make sure that their soil is always damp. After a few weeks they should start to grow, showing that they have taken root.

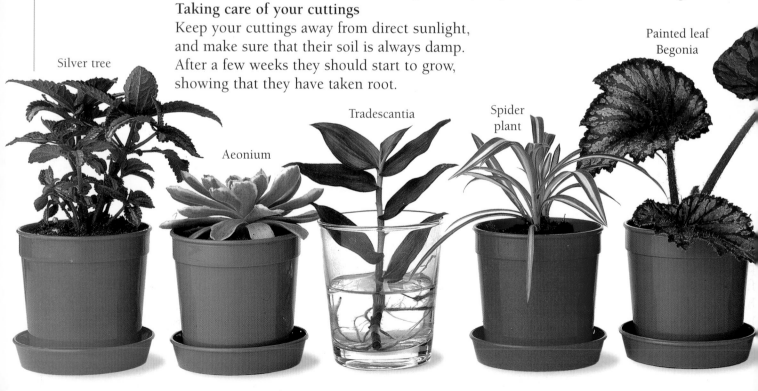

Silver tree

Aeonium

Tradescantia

Spider plant

Painted leaf Begonia

44 Grow cress heads

Here is a growing experiment that turns plants into an unusual kind of hair! The "hair" is made of cress seedlings, and grows out of eggshell "flowerpots" that have their own painted faces. If you keep your cress heads well watered, their hair will stand on end. But if you forget to water them, the cotton wool will dry out, and their hair will start to flop in all different directions.

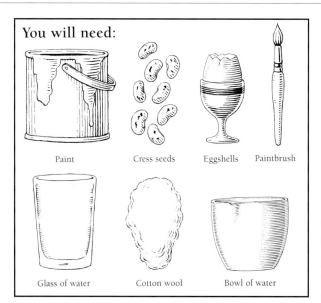

You will need:

Paint   Cress seeds   Eggshells   Paintbrush

Glass of water   Cotton wool   Bowl of water

A handful of cress seeds

Undecorated eggshell

1. Collect some halves of empty eggshells. Using a small brush, paint a face on each shell. Be sure to hold the shells gently, or you might break them.

2. Break off a small piece of cotton wool. Moisten it in a bowl of water, and squeeze out any excess liquid before you put it in the eggshell.

3. Scatter the cress seeds on the surface of the damp cotton wool. Then put your cress seeds somewhere light and warm, and watch "hair" slowly grow.

Hair will grow in just a few days

Keep cotton wool moist

4. If you look at the experiment on page 30, you will find out why the hair will not grow back if you decide to give it a trim.

45 Make a mini-desert

In deserts, months go by without rain, and the sunshine is fierce. Desert plants survive by having deep roots and storing water in their fleshy stems. If you have a warm and sunny window sill, you can make a desert of your own. Desert plants are easy to look after because they do not need much water.

1. Using a trowel cover the bottom of the planting tray with a layer of gravel. Then fill with soil until it is about half full.

Planting tray

Gravel or coarse pebbles

Coarse sand

Soil or potting compost

2. Before taking the plants out of their pots, move them around in the tray, until you have found the best arrangement.

3. Using a trowel, dig a hole for each plant. Carefully remove each plant from its pot. Loosen the soil around the roots and carefully plant them.

Propeller plant   Haworthia   Christmas cactus   Finger-mound cactus   Fish-hook cactus   Thimble cactus

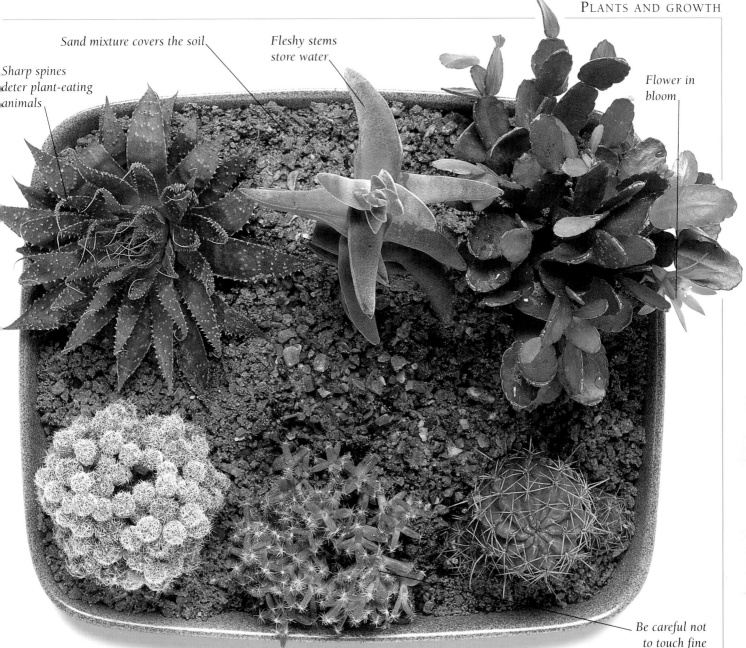

Sand mixture covers the soil

Fleshy stems store water

Sharp spines deter plant-eating animals

Flower in bloom

Be careful not to touch fine hair-like spines

4. Using a spoon fill the gaps between each plant with soil. Check that all the plant's roots are completely covered.

5. Gently spoon the sand mixture over the compost and press it down firmly with the back of a spoon.

6. Your mini-desert is now complete. Your plants will need watering about once a week, but be careful not to let the soil get too wet.

43

46 Create a window garden

With your own window garden, you can watch plants closely, to see how they grow and flower. Planting a window garden is quite easy. Before you begin, decide which plants you would like to grow. Try to avoid plants that grow too big. Look for plants with small leaves because they cope better with bright sunlight and sudden gusts of wind. If your window ledge slopes, place some small pieces of wood under the front of the window box to keep it level.

You will need:

Window box and tray

Water sprayer

Trowel

Scissors

Soil or potting compost
Gravel or coarse pebbles
PLUS Assorted small flowering plants

Watering can

Pansy

Chrysanthemum

Gravel or coarse pebbles

Soil

Impatiens will stay in flower most of the summer

Drip tray collects excess water

1. Using the trowel, cover the bottom of the window box with a layer of gravel. Then fill the window box with soil until it is about three-quarters full.

2. Decide how you want to arrange the plants. The tallest plants should go at the back, and trailing plants at the front.

Bellflower

Impatiens

3. Remember where the plants go, and then carefully remove each one from its pot. Gently loosen the roots by pinching at the soil with your fingertips.

4. Dig a hole, and lower the plant into it. Using your knuckles, press around the plant, make sure it is firmly embedded in the soil and that the roots have enough room.

5. Add the rest of the plants until the window box is full, but leave enough room for watering. Take care not to snap any of the stems.

Chrysanthemum are noted for their varied colours

If you regularly remove dead flower heads, the plants will flower for longer

Spray the flowers with water to keep them fresh

Food and drink
Unlike a mini-desert (see pages 42–43), your window box will need plenty of water. You may want to use some liquid plant food as well.

Bellflower will bloom from late summer until early winter

47 Design a butterfly garden

Butterflies are busy animals that are always on the lookout for food. They drink a sugary liquid called nectar, which they collect when they visit sweet-smelling flowers. Try planting some of the nectar-rich flowers below in a window box, or if you have room, grow some in a corner of the garden. Leave them in a sunny spot and you will attract an assortment of butterflies in the late summer months.

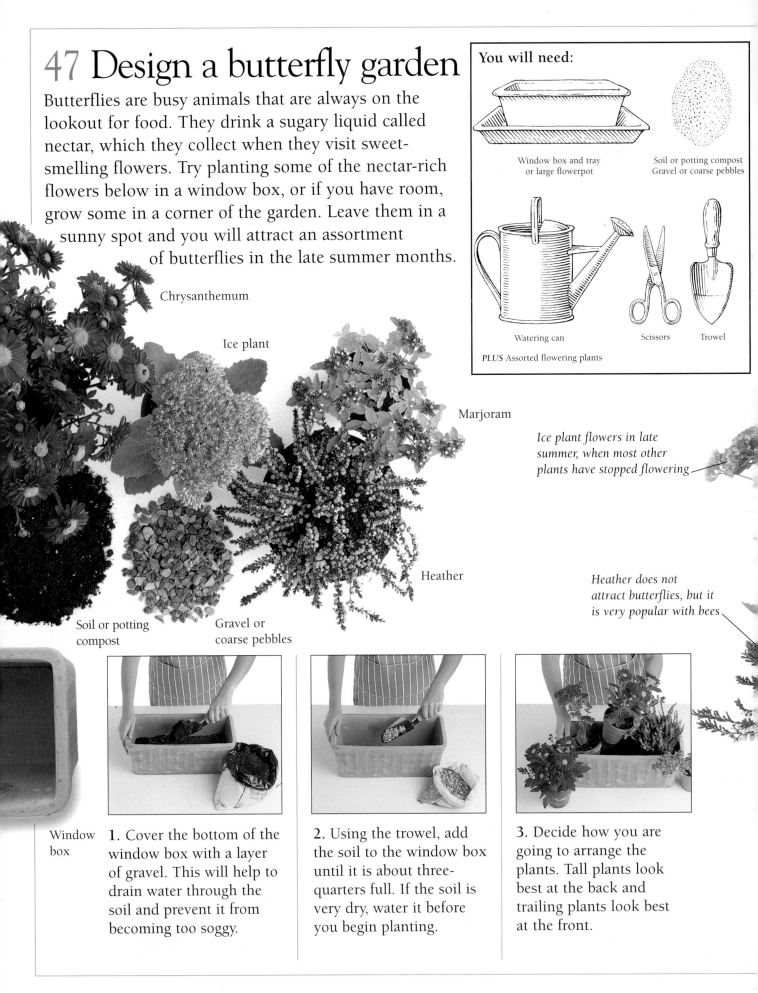

You will need:

Window box and tray or large flowerpot

Soil or potting compost
Gravel or coarse pebbles

Watering can

Scissors

Trowel

PLUS Assorted flowering plants

Chrysanthemum

Ice plant

Marjoram

Ice plant flowers in late summer, when most other plants have stopped flowering

Heather

Soil or potting compost

Gravel or coarse pebbles

Heather does not attract butterflies, but it is very popular with bees

Window box

1. Cover the bottom of the window box with a layer of gravel. This will help to drain water through the soil and prevent it from becoming too soggy.

2. Using the trowel, add the soil to the window box until it is about three-quarters full. If the soil is very dry, water it before you begin planting.

3. Decide how you are going to arrange the plants. Tall plants look best at the back and trailing plants look best at the front.

4. Turn the first flowerpot upside down and gently ease the plant out. Loosen its roots by pinching at the soil.

5. Dig a hole and then lower the plant into it. Make sure that the soil around the plant is firm. Remember to water the flowers every day in hot weather.

Blooming attraction

When the plants are in full bloom, their scent and bright colours will attract hungry butterflies and other insects. When you see a butterfly arrive, watch it closely. With luck, you may be able to see its long tongue uncoil and probe into the flowers. A butterfly's tongue works like a drinking straw, sucking up nectar into its mouth.

The flat shape of these daisy-like flowers makes an ideal landing platform for a butterfly

Marjoram is a strong-scented herb that attracts bees and butterflies

Terracotta window box

48 Grow a salad garden

Here is an easy way to make an instant salad garden by simply growing salad seeds in dampened cotton wool. You can grow anything that will sprout quickly – cress, radish, and lettuce seeds will sprout in a few days and be ready to eat in a week. The seeds will sprout all year round, but they must be left in a light spot such as a sunny windowsill. Salad plants contain substances called vitamins, which are essential to keep your body healthy and strong.

You will need:

Water sprayer

3 glass jars

Jug of water

3 saucers

Labels

Sieve

Assorted salad seeds

Cotton wool

3 polythene bags

1. Put the seeds in a sieve and rinse them under a tap of cold water. Half-fill the glass jars with water and add seeds. Leave them to stand for about four hours, so they are thoroughly wet.

Cress seeds

Mung bean seeds

2. Place a layer of cotton wool on each of the saucers. This will give the plants something to anchor their roots into as soon as they start growing. Then fetch a jug of water.

3. Pour some water into each saucer of cotton wool. Make sure that the cotton wool becomes wet. But do not pour too much water on the cotton wool as this will prevent growth.

4. Fetch the seeds and use the sieve to drain the seeds from each jar. Then spread them out evenly on top of the wet cotton wool so they have enough room for growth.

5. In order for the seeds to germinate they must be kept wet. Spray them with plenty of water so that they remain damp.

6. Place each saucer inside a polythene bag and label them. This will stop the seeds from drying out. Leave the saucers somewhere warm, such as on a sunny windowsill.

7. In a few days, your seeds will germinate (begin growing). When this happens take the saucers out of their polythene bags and spray the seedlings to keep them wet. As soon as the seedlings are high enough, you can harvest them with a pair of scissors.

What happens next?
Your salad garden will not keep growing forever. Even if you keep watering the seedlings, they will eventually start to turn yellow and wither. Seedlings can begin growing without soil, but they need to grow in soil to remain healthy.

Two-day-old mung bean seeds

Two-day old cress seeds

Cress seeds are ready to be harvested

Mung bean seeds after seven days

Cress seeds after seven days

Check the progress of your salad plants daily

FLOWERS

FLOWERS ARE THE PARTS OF PLANTS that make seeds. They produce a substance called pollen, which is carried from one flower to another. Every flower has a special shape and colour. Some are small and green, and spread pollen with the help of the wind. Others are big and bright, and have a delicious smell. They spread pollen with the help of insects and other animals.

49 Dissect a flower

From a distance, flowers often look just like clusters of colourful petals. But there is much more to a flower than just its petals. In this experiment you will use a scalpel to carefully reveal all the parts of a flower that make up the pollen and seeds. Then you can examine them with a magnifying glass.

You will need:

Scissors Magnifying glass Scalpel Tweezers
PLUS Poppy, Buttercup, Tulip, or Lily

Adult supervision is essential

Poppy petals

How many petals?
Each plant family has flowers with a characteristic number of petals. Like most plants in the poppy family this poppy has four petals.

Petal

Receptacle

Stigma

Seeds form in the ovaries

1. Cut off any green flaps at the back of the flower, and then use the scalpel to slice off the petals where they join the stalk. This will leave you with the centre of the flower.

2. Carefully trim away the stalk-like stamens, and look at them with the magnifying glass. The tips of the stamens are called anthers and they make the flower's pollen. They brush the pollen onto insects or other animals that visit the flower.

3. You should now be left with the parts of the flower that make the seeds. They collect pollen from the visiting insects and other animals that help to scatter the seeds when they are ripe. If you cut open this part of the flower, you may see the seeds inside.

50 Press some flowers

Some flowers bloom for a few hours, while others last for many weeks. Eventually, their petals wither away. If you collect some flowers and press them, you can preserve your flowers for as long as you like. Pressing works best with small, freshly picked flowers.

You will need:

Blotting paper

Books or heavy wooden boards
PLUS Small flowers

1. Put a thick sheet of blotting paper on a book or board. Arrange the flowers on the paper, and then cover them with another sheet of paper.

2. Add a heavy weight, such as a pile of books. Leave the flowers for a week so they become squashed and dried. Carefully lift up the blotting paper and arrange the flowers how you want them. Remember they are fragile, so you must handle them with care.

51 Seeing colours

Flowers get their colours from pigments in their petals. If you dissolve some flowers you will see many pigments.

Adult supervision is essential

You will need:

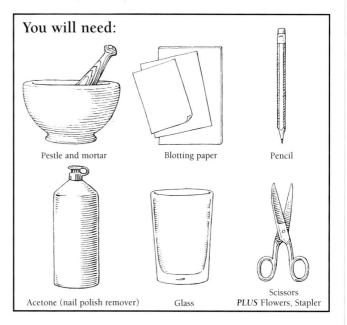

Pestle and mortar

Blotting paper

Pencil

Acetone (nail polish remover)

Glass

Scissors
PLUS Flowers, Stapler

1. Put flowers in a mortar and add 20 ml (4 tsp) of acetone. Grind the mixture with the pestle and put it into a glass. Staple a strip of blotting paper around a pencil and let it hang so it touches the mixture.

Blotting paper soaks up liquid

Each colour you see is a pigment

2. Leave it for one hour in a well-ventilated room. The acetone will slowly creep up the blotting paper and separate into bands of different colour.

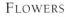

Cut the stems to make the flowers the same length

Tie the string tight

52 Make a dried flower arrangement

You will need:

Scissors

String

PLUS Fresh flowers

When you keep fresh flowers in water they do not last for long, but if you dry fresh flowers you can make them last much longer. You can press flowers (see page 51), which flattens them while drying, or you can hang them upside down in a warm place, which will preserve the flowers' colour and shape.

String

1. Lay the flowers out on a tabletop, and cut their stems so they are all the same length. Arrange the flowers in a bundle, and tie them up with some string. Make sure the string is tight because the stems shrink as they dry out. Hang up the flowers somewhere warm and dry.

Roses have a strong scent

2. After two weeks, the flowers and leaves will have completely dried out. Cut the string and carefully arrange the flowers in a vase. Place the arrangement where everyone can admire it.

Gypsophila has small white or pink flowers

The arrangement takes around two weeks to dry

53 Preserve flowers

This method of drying flowers is more complicated than the one opposite, but it sometimes gives better results. It uses a substance called silica gel, which absorbs the moisture in flowers. As it absorbs moisture, the gel turns from blue to pink. You can dry it out again by baking it in an oven at a low temperature.

👫 *Adult supervision is advised*

1. Put a layer of silica gel into a large jar. Then place some flowers upside down in the jar. Make sure that the flowers are well spread out.

The colour of some flowers may fade

Tallest stems are placed in the centre of the arrangement

Dried roses often keep their scent and shape

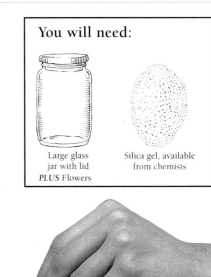

You will need:

Large glass jar with lid
PLUS Flowers

Silica gel, available from chemists

Place the flowers upside down

Silica gel

Pour the silica gel carefully into the jar

2. Slowly add more silica gel, until the flowers are completely covered. Gently tap the jar to remove any air spaces, and then screw the lid onto the jar. Leave the flowers in the jar for at least a week to dry.

Leave the flowers for at least a week

53

TREES

WOULDN'T IT BE HARD to imagine a world without trees? They are the longest-living plants on dry land, and the biggest. Trees are the most important components of a forest, because they provide food and shelter for all kinds of animals from ants to elephants. They also support woodland fungi which feed either on living trees, on dead wood, or fallen leaves.

54 See buds burst

Some trees keep their leaves all year round. Others shed them in autumn, and grow a completely new set in spring. The new leaves actually start to develop in the previous year, but then spend the winter packed inside the buds. When spring arrives, the buds burst and the new leaves start to grow. You can make buds open early by cutting some twigs and bringing them indoors. Put them in a jar of water and give them plenty of warmth and sunlight.

You will need:

Water
Jar
Pruning shears
PLUS Twigs (horse chestnuts, poplars, and willows are best)

Flower bud

New leaves inside the bud begin to unfold

Leaf scar

Each flower bud is covered with sticky scales that protect it

Flower bud

New shoot

Girdle scar

Soon, bud scales will drop off, leaving a girdle scar

Keep the twigs in clean water

In early spring, look out for twigs with buds that are beginning to swell. Cut them off, and then put them in water in a well-lit spot such as a sunny windowsill. As the days pass, the leaves inside begin to grow and you will see the bud's outer scales fold back. Eventually, new shoots will break out of the buds and the leaves will begin to unfold.

55 Discover the age of a tree

Trees grow at different rates. By measuring around their trunks you can get a guide to their age. Palm trees and some fast-growing trees, such as conifers and eucalyptuses, do not follow this rule.

You will need:

Tape measure

Pencil   Notebook

The circumference of a mature tree increases by 2.5 cm (1 in) every year

1. Hold the tape measure at a height of at least 1 m (3 ft) above the ground and then measure the tree's circumference.

2. Divide the measurement by 2.5 cm (1 in) to discover the tree's approximate age in years.

56 Measure the height of a tree

Guessing the height of a tree can be difficult, because it is hard to compare a tree with anything nearby. Here is an easy way to come up with an accurate answer. To try it out, you will need a friend to help.

You will need:

Measuring tape

Pencil   Notebook
PLUS A stick

The top lines up with the top of your friend's head

Pencil mark lines up with friend's feet

Friend standing under a tree

Stick must be held at arm's length

1. Measure the height of your friend and write it down in your notebook. Then ask him or her to stand at the base of a tree.

2. Hold the stick at arm's length and line up the top of the stick with the top of your friend's head. Then mark the stick where it lines up with your friend's feet.

3. Now see how many times you can fit the marked length of the stick into the height of the tree. Multiply this number with the height of your friend to calculate the height of the tree.

57 Plant a tree

During the autumn months, lots of trees drop their leaves and seeds onto the ground. Some seeds germinate (begin growing) a few days after leaving the tree. Others take much longer to grow because they wait until the cold winter weather has passed. If you collect some seeds, you can plant them in pots and watch them grow.

You will need:

3 flowerpots

Jug of water

Pen

Plant labels

Trowel

Assorted tree seeds

Watering can

Soil or potting compost
Gravel or coarse pebbles

1. Put a small amount of gravel into each flowerpot, this will help the water drain away. Fill the rest of each pot with soil.

Acorns

Sycamore seeds

Horse chestnuts

Sweet chestnuts

2. Plant a different seed in each flowerpot. Push the seeds down in the soil, and cover them up. Water the soil until it is thoroughly wet.

3. Label each flowerpot with the tree's name. Put the flowerpots somewhere cool and shady (outside is best), and wait for the seeds to start growing.

As the tree grows, its stem becomes much stronger

Growing sycamore
Once the tree reaches between 10 cm (3.9 in) and 12 cm (4.7 in), take it out of the flowerpot and plant it in a sunny spot.

58 Make a bark rubbing

Some bark is smooth, but other kinds of bark are rough and full of cracks. If you attach some strong paper to a tree trunk with masking tape and rub it firmly with a wax crayon, you can make a "rubbing" of the bark.

Make a collection of rubbings from different trees and notice how the patterns vary

Rub firmly over the trunk

You will need:

Masking tape

Crayons

Paper

59 Make a leaf skeleton

When the soft parts of dead leaves rot away they leave behind a "skeleton" of veins. You can find plenty of leaf skeletons on the ground in autumn. In this experiment you will make them at home by using washing soda, which gently dissolves the soft parts of a leaf.

👥 *Adult supervision is essential*

You will need:

Pan of water

PLUS Fallen leaves   Washing soda

Veins

Midrib

Stalk

Dead leaf

1. Dissolve some washing soda in a small pan of water. Add the leaves and then gently warm the pan. Do not let it get too hot.

2. Take the pan away from the heat, and leave it for several hours. Remove the leaf skeletons, and rinse them thoroughly.

60 Grow mould

Moulds do not grow from seeds. Instead, they grow when a spore (dustlike speck), lands on something it can digest. The spore then breaks open, and starts to grow. In this experiment you will see what happens when mould spores land on three slices of bread that are prepared in different ways.

You will need:

Food wrap

Antiseptic disinfectant

Container

PLUS 3 slices of bread

Jug of water

1. Put two slices of bread in a container. Leave the third slice out so it will become dry.

2. Try not to let the slices of bread touch. Pour a small amount of disinfectant onto one of the slices. Be careful not to get any on the neighbouring slice.

3. Pour enough water on both slices of bread to make them quite damp. But you must be careful not to let any of the water build up in the base of the container.

4. Seal the container with food wrap. This will shut in any spores that have fallen on the bread, and keep it damp. Put all three slices somewhere dark and warm.

Mould has grown on the damp bread

The disinfectant kills the spores so no mould can grow

5. After three days, look at the result. The damp bread will probably show signs of mould. The dry bread and the disinfected bread have no mould.

Moisture and warmth help the mould feed on the bread

Dry bread has no mould

61 Make a spore print

Mushrooms and toadstools drop tiny spores in the air, enabling fungi to spread. Normally, the wind carries spores far and wide. In this experiment, you will use the spores to make a special print. Remember to wash your hands after touching wild toadstools.

You will need:

Plastic bowl | Coloured card
PLUS Mushroom or toadstool caps with dark undersides, Spray fixative

1. Slice off a mushroom's stalk, and put the cap on a piece of card. Cover it with a bowl to prevent the spores from being blown away.

2. The next day, carefully lift off the mushroom's cap. The mushroom's spores will have now fallen onto the card and made a print.

3. To stop the spores from smudging, spray the print with fixative, such as hairspray. When the hairspray is dry, your print will be finished.

Use different coloured cards

Collect prints of other mushrooms

The spores fall from underneath the mushroom cap

62 Make a woodland terrarium

A terrarium is a home for keeping small animals that live on land. It contains food for them to eat, fresh water for them to drink, and places for them to hide. In this experiment you will find out how to make a terrarium especially suited to small woodland animals. Once you have filled it with dead branches, leaf mould, and a few beetles and woodlice it will resemble a small area of woodland floor.

You will need:

Aquarium tank with lid

Shallow bowl

Soil

Trowel

Water sprayer

Small dead branches
Pine cones

PLUS Leaf mould, Small animals
(Beetles, Woodlice, Millipedes, and Snails)

Small dead branch

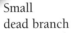
Soil

Pine cones

Leaf mould

1. Fill one corner of the tank with some dead leaves and wood. This will provide a place for the animals to climb onto and hide.

2. Fill the remainder of the tank floor with soil, and add some pine cones. Place the bowl in the soil, and fill it with water.

3. Add more soil around the bowl to keep it in place. Sprinkle some water over the tank to keep it damp.

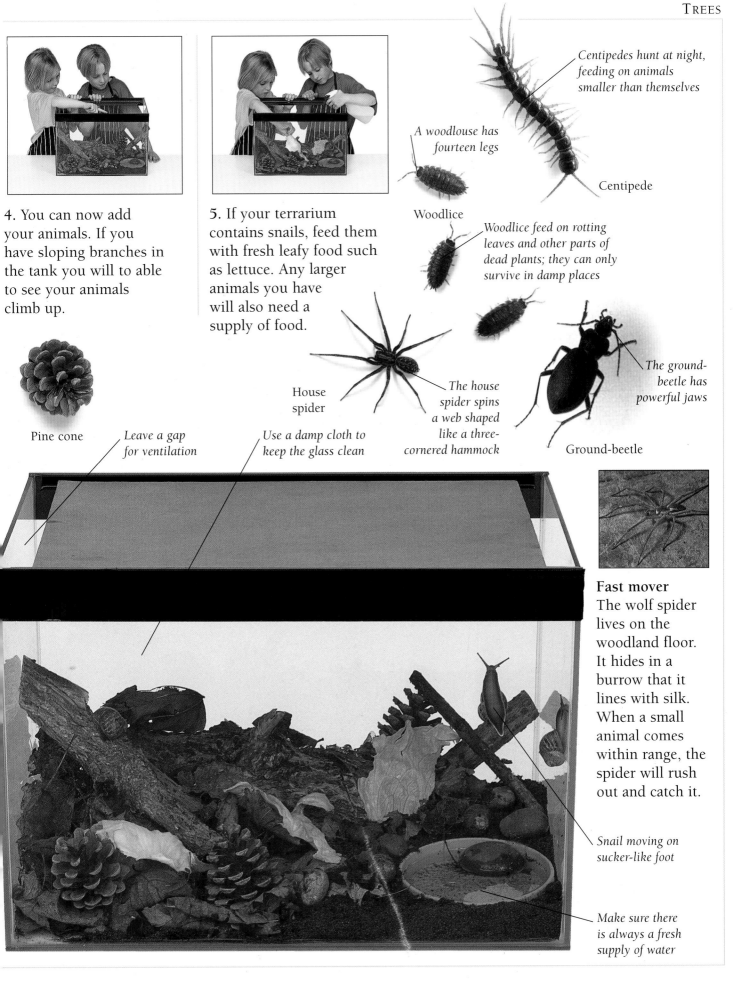

4. You can now add your animals. If you have sloping branches in the tank you will to able to see your animals climb up.

5. If your terrarium contains snails, feed them with fresh leafy food such as lettuce. Any larger animals you have will also need a supply of food.

Centipedes hunt at night, feeding on animals smaller than themselves

Centipede

A woodlouse has fourteen legs

Woodlice

Woodlice feed on rotting leaves and other parts of dead plants; they can only survive in damp places

Pine cone

Leave a gap for ventilation

Use a damp cloth to keep the glass clean

House spider

The house spider spins a web shaped like a three-cornered hammock

The ground-beetle has powerful jaws

Ground-beetle

Fast mover
The wolf spider lives on the woodland floor. It hides in a burrow that it lines with silk. When a small animal comes within range, the spider will rush out and catch it.

Snail moving on sucker-like foot

Make sure there is always a fresh supply of water

61

SMALL ANIMALS

ABOUT TWO MILLION different kinds of animals have been discovered on Earth. Animals range from tiny, simple creatures to gigantic blue whales. The vast majority of animals are small or tiny, and they include over one million species of insects and 30,000 different species of spiders.

63 Look at insects close up

In spring and summer, trees play host to a huge number of insects. Some eat leaves or sap, while others are hunters that search the tree for prey. Even if you stand close to a tree, few of these insects are easy to see. But with the help of a beater tray you will be able to see tree-dwelling insects close up.

You will need:

Drawing pins

Square of white fabric
PLUS Stick

Wooden frame
(see pp. 12–13)

Assemble the frame

1. The frame used here is the same as for the quadrat on pages 12–13. Once you have assembled the frame, stretch the fabric over it, and use the drawing pins to fasten it in position.

2. Hold the tray under a low, leafy branch, and hit the branch several times with a stick (be careful not to break the branch). The insects will lose their grip, and tumble onto the tray. If you want you can repeat the experiment with different trees.

Watch out for escaping insects

Animal life comes tumbling onto the tray

64 Make a "pooter"

A pooter is a special device that allows you to pick up fast-moving, small animals without touching or harming them. The pooter works by suction. You suck through one tube and the animals are drawn up through another tube into the jar.

You will need:

Glass jar with lid   Screwdriver   Wire   Sticky tape

PLUS Modelling clay   Muslin   3 ballpoint pen barrels   Rubber pipe   Rubber band

1. Make two holes in the jar's lid with a screwdriver. Cover one end of a pen barrel with muslin. Push the pen barrels through each hole. Seal them both in position with modelling clay.

2. Fit a piece of rubber pipe to the outer end of each pen barrel. Bend the rubber pipe connected to the barrel without muslin (you can make it bend by taping wires to it). Add the third barrel to the outer end of the bent pipe. Screw on the lid.

Suction through pipe

Muslin stops insects from going into your mouth

65 Test a worm's reaction

A worm's tail is extremely sensitive to touch. If a bird touches a worm's tail, the worm will suddenly contract (squeeze up), and pull its whole body underground in order to escape. If you collect an earthworm and lightly touch its tail, you can see what happens.

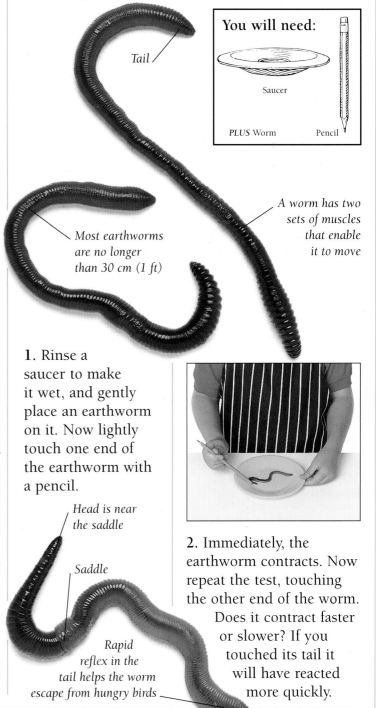

Tail

You will need:

Saucer

PLUS Worm   Pencil

A worm has two sets of muscles that enable it to move

Most earthworms are no longer than 30 cm (1 ft)

1. Rinse a saucer to make it wet, and gently place an earthworm on it. Now lightly touch one end of the earthworm with a pencil.

Head is near the saddle

Saddle

Rapid reflex in the tail helps the worm escape from hungry birds

2. Immediately, the earthworm contracts. Now repeat the test, touching the other end of the worm. Does it contract faster or slower? If you touched its tail it will have reacted more quickly.

66 Build a caterpillar house

Have you ever watched a caterpillar change into a butterfly? If you make your own caterpillar house you may be lucky enough to see this happen. The best time to collect caterpillars is early spring or summer. Caterpillars are choosy eaters, so make sure you always feed them with the same kind of leaves you found them living on in the wild.

Adult supervision is essential

Some caterpillars have tufts or bristles that irritate the skin, so always pick them up with a paintbrush

Feed your caterpillars with fresh leaves every day

Twig

A caterpillar changes into a chrysalis (or pupa) when it is fully grown

5. After a few weeks, you may see the caterpillars change into chrysalises and then into adult butterflies.

Do not prod or disturb the caterpillars because they are very delicate

Set your butterfly free when it is sunny

1. Ask an adult to cut around the box's lid, so just the rim is left behind. Cut out a piece of muslin big enough to cover the box.

2. Line the box with kitchen paper, and spray it with water until it feels slightly damp. This stops the caterpillars from drying out.

3. Put some twigs in the box and add some leaves. Use the paintbrush to pick up the caterpillars and place them on the leaves.

A caterpillar will moult several times during its life

4. Put some muslin over the box. Then push the lid down over the muslin to hold it firmly in place. The house is now complete

67 Make a bee nestbox

Bumblebees are big, furry bees that start flying early in the year. Female bumblebees lay their eggs in small nests, which they often build underground. Instead of digging a hole, the bumblebee will look for one that has already been made. Nesting sites are often in short supply. If you make the special nestbox shown here, you can help a bumblebee set up home.

You will need:

Small flowerpot with central drainage hole

4 corks

Wood shavings or sawdust

Wooden cover 12 cm x 12 cm (5 in x 5 in)

Dig a hole in the ground and fill it with a small heap of sawdust or wood shavings. Place the pot upside down, inside the hole, so the drainage hole is level with the ground. Place the wooden cover on the corks, so that a bee is able to crawl underneath.

Build your nest in early spring

68 Train honeybees

In spring and summer honeybees fly from flower to flower to collect a sugary liquid called nectar. They use the nectar as food, and take it back to their nests. When a bee arrives at the nest it tells other bees where it can be found. In this experiment, you will train honeybees to come to an artificial flower with a sugary liquid centre. As you can see here, lots of bees will soon arrive to feed.

You will need:

Sugar

Jug of warm water
PLUS 5 identical bottletops

Coloured cardboard

1. Cut out five identical "flowers" from different coloured card. Put the bottletops in the centre of the flowers. Now add some sugary liquid to one of the flowers.

Sugary liquid

2. If the weather is warm, a honeybee will soon arrive to investigate the flower and discover the food. After it has flown off, other bees will begin to arrive.

3. Within a short time, lots of bees will be busy feeding at the same flower. They use their long tongues to lap up the sugary water.

Once a bee has found food it fetches other bees

"Flower" is crowded with bees

4. Soon the bees are jostling for space. It is quite safe to watch them, but do not disturb them while they are feeding.

69 On the move

Life is full of choices for all animals. They have to choose whether to go in one direction or another, what to eat, and where to hide. The study of animal behaviour in nature is known as ethology, and is based on observing the many choices an animal makes. Even simple animals such as woodlice can behave in quite a complex way. In this experiment you will see how woodlice decide between two sets of conditions – dry or moist and light or dark.

Adult supervision is essential

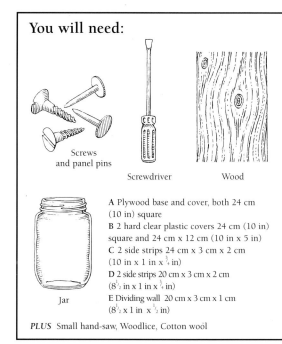

You will need:

Screws and panel pins

Screwdriver

Wood

Jar

A Plywood base and cover, both 24 cm (10 in) square
B 2 hard clear plastic covers 24 cm (10 in) square and 24 cm x 12 cm (10 in x 5 in)
C 2 side strips 24 cm x 3 cm x 2 cm (10 in x 1 in x $\frac{3}{4}$ in)
D 2 side strips 20 cm x 3 cm x 2 cm (8$\frac{1}{2}$ in x 1 in x $\frac{3}{4}$ in)
E Dividing wall 20 cm x 3 cm x 1 cm (8$\frac{1}{2}$ x 1 in x $\frac{1}{2}$ in)

PLUS Small hand-saw, Woodlice, Cotton wool

E

A

C

B

D

1. Screw the side strips (C and D) to the base (A), and cut three openings in the dividing wall (E). Make them large enough so the insects can crawl through. Fix the dividing wall to the base so it splits the space into two equal chambers.

2. Collect some woodlice (you will find them outside under stones or pieces of wood). Distribute them into each of the chambers. Leave them for at least ten minutes so they are able get used to their new home.

Woodlice move from one compartment to the other through the small doorway

Collect woodlice in a jar and place them into the chamber

3. To see if woodlice prefer dry or moist surroundings, place a piece of moistened cotton wool in one of the compartments and cover the whole box. The following day, see how the woodlice are distributed. You will find that most of the woodlice are in the compartment containing cotton wool. This is because they prefer moist conditions.

4. To see if woodlice prefer light or dark conditions, cover one compartment with clear plastic (B), and the other with the wooden lid (A). After four to six hours, see where the woodlice are. You will find that most of them have chosen to remain in the covered compartment. This is because woodlice normally feed after dark, and do not like daylight.

*A woodlouse
is harmless*

70 Nature's night shift

At night, when it is cool and damp, all sorts of animals come out in search of food. In this experiment you will make an animal shelter from a grapefruit to attract some of these wandering creatures of the night. Leave it overnight, and in the morning you can see what you have caught.

You will need:

Chopping board   Knife   Spoon
PLUS Grapefruit

1. Slice the grapefruit in half. Remove the fleshy fruit with the spoon so you are left with only the skin.

Woodlouse

2. Place the grapefruit skins outside, hollow side down, on some bare ground. The skins are tough and full of juice. The juice will make the air underneath the fruit moist and attract lots of animals.

Midnight feast
Slugs come out at night searching for food. This slug has discovered a plum that has fallen from a tree onto the ground.

3. Leave the skins overnight, and then turn them over to see how many different animals have gathered beneath.

Slug

71 Make a spider's web

Many spiders capture flying insects by spinning a silken web. A spider's web looks delicate, but the silk of some webs can be stronger than steel wire of the same thickness. A spider builds a sticky spiral out of liquid silk that it squeezes out of its body. As soon as the silk meets the air it hardens. You can make your own web with some string and pins.

You will need:

Scissors   Thick cardboard   Pins   String   Pencil

1. Cut out a square of cardboard. Each side should be 30 cm (12 in) in length. Mark the centre of the cardboard and then draw lines through it.

It takes a spider about one hour to spin a web like this

A real spider's web is made from liquid silk

5. Your web is now complete. When a spider has finished its web, it waits in the centre for an insect to get caught. As soon as a victim lands in the sticky web, the thread shakes, and the spider moves to attack.

2. Place a pin at the top of each line so you create a large circle. Repeat with the remaining pins so you make smaller circles. Continue until you reach the centre of the cardboard.

3. Tie a piece of string, as neatly as possible, from one end of the outer pins (across the centre) to the other end. Continue until all the outer pins have string running across them.

4. Pick up the ball of string. Carefully weave a spiral outwards from the centre of the web until you reach the edge. A real spider would spiral back into the centre.

Recycled silk
Spiders often have to repair their webs. When a web is damaged, a spider eats it, and then weaves a new one. In this way, it recycles its silk.

72 Make a moth trap

Moths are often attracted to bright lights, which is why they sometimes flutter into lit rooms through open windows after dark. Moths are quite harmless. Most have short wings, and stubby bodies. If you want to get a closer look at some night-flying moths, try making the simple moth trap shown here.

Adult supervision is advised

You will need:

Shoe box · Funnel · Sharp knife · Angle desk lamp

1. Carefully cut through the funnel with a sharp knife, so that a hole at least 2.5 cm (1 in) wide is left at the narrow end.

2. Cut a hole in the top of the shoe box, wider than the narrow end of the funnel. The funnel should sit upright in the hole.

3. After dark, put the shoe box outside. Keep it away from bright lights such as street lamps so the moths are not distracted.

Male oak eggar
Male moths often have feathery antennae (feelers).

Front wing

Clever disguise
The lappet moth folds its wings over its body to resemble dead leaves.

Hind wing

Female lobster moth
This moth's caterpillar has a tail like a lobster's.

Abdomen

Bright light attracts moths

If you make the hole in the funnel and the shoe box wider, you will trap larger moths

4. Put the funnel in position and plug in the lamp. Lower the lamp so that it is about 20 cm (8 in) above the funnel, and switch it on. Leave it for one or two hours. Then pull the box away from the lamp, and carefully lift the lid. Your moths should be sitting inside.

69

73 Track animals

Many wild animals are naturally shy, and will quickly run away if they hear you coming. But if you look carefully on the ground, you can sometimes find the tracks that these animals leave behind. The shape of the tracks and the way they fit together, can often tell you what animal has made them. Tracks form best on soft ground or snow. Use the special track tray shown here, and you will see tracks formed in sand.

You will need:

Glass jar

Fine sand

Tray

Ruler

Sand with very fine grains produces the clearest results

Tiger feet
These tracks were made by a tiger walking across soft mud. Domestic cat tracks look almos exactly the same, but smaller.

1. Pour the sand into the tray, or directly onto the ground. Make it slightly damp with a little water to ensure that it does not move around after an animal has stepped on it.

2. Drag the ruler across the sand to give it a smooth, flat surface. If you are using a tray, place it outside in the ground so that it is level with the soil around it.

3. First thing in the morning, check the sand for tracks. If any are there, see if you can work out which animal they belong to. Small, round paw prints, without claw marks, are often made by cats. Bigger prints, with claw marks, are made by raccoons, badgers, and other nocturnal animals. If the tracks are evenly spaced, the animal that made them was probaby walking or running. If they are in pairs, it was hopping.

74 Make a plaster cast

In the wild, tracks do not last for long. They disappear as the wind blows, or as rain washes across the soil. But with the help of some quick-setting plaster of Paris, you can keep a permanent collection of any tracks that you find. This method works best on damp sand and mud. It does not work in snow, because the liquid plaster is warm before it becomes solid, and it will melt the tracks.

You will need:

Mixing bowl   Paper clips

Spoon   Plaster of Paris   Scissors

Cardboard   Jug

1. Once you have located some tracks, gently brush away any leaves or twigs around them. Pick out any pieces of mud that have fallen into the tracks so that you have a clean print.

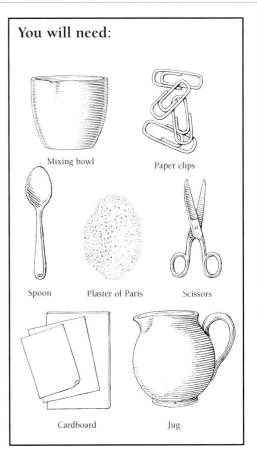

Raised casts of deer tracks

2. Use the paper clips to fasten a strip of cardboard into a ring slightly bigger than the tracks. Position the ring around the tracks, and then press it gently into the soil about 1 cm (¹/₂ in) deep. Make sure there are no gaps around the bottom of the ring through which the liquid plaster could flow out.

3. Mix up some plaster, adding water a little bit at a time until it is like runny cream. Pour the liquid mixture into the cardboard ring and smooth the surface. Wait for it to set, which will take about an hour. When the plaster is firm to the touch, lift it up, with the cardboard ring still attached to it.

4. Let the plaster dry out for at least a day. Once it is dry, remove the cardboard. The tracks stick out of the plaster, but otherwise they are just like the ones in the ground. Collect plaster casts of different tracks and compare them.

75 Track snails

When studying wild animals, it is useful to find out where they go. Marking animals can show how far they travel, and keep track of how many there are. In this experiment you will do some wildlife tracking in your own garden or backyard.

You will need:

Flowerpot

Paintbrush

Enamel paint
PLUS Garden snails

1. Pick up each snail, and tap it to make it pull in its body. Using the paintbrush, mark a number on the shell, taking care not to get any paint on the snail's body.

Number identifies each snail

2. Put the snails in the flowerpot, and then see where you find them on the following days. What is the farthest distance that they travel from their home?

A large clay flowerpot makes an ideal home for snails

Snails rest in damp places

76 Observe fruit flies

Insects live on an amazing variety of different foods. Some feed on plants, some chew their way through wool, some even drink blood! In this experiment, you can observe tiny flies that feed on fruit. In summer, fruit flies wander through the air, searching for a suitable place to lay their eggs.

You will need:

Square piece of cloth   Elastic band   Knife

Glass jar
PLUS Chopping board, Banana

Adult supervision is advised

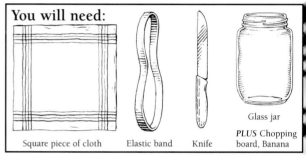

1. Choose a banana that is thoroughly ripe. The smell of the banana will attract female fruit flies that are ready to lay eggs.

Cover the bananas after a few days

Leave the bananas in a warm and bright place

DAY 2

2. Cut the banana into pieces that are 2.5 cm (1 in) long. Fruit flies do not worry about the skin, so there is no need to peel it first.

3. Put the pieces of banana in the jar. Leave it uncovered and put it in a warm and bright place until the banana begins to turn black.

4. Fasten the fabric over the jar with the elastic band. Keep the jar in a warm and bright place, and check it every day for any signs of change.

Fruit feast
The fruit flies shown on this banana are magnified. However, you will need good eyesight to spot them. They are only about 3 mm ($^1/_{10}$ in) long!

Fruit flies hatch in only ten days

Fabric over the jar will stop the flies from escaping

5. If the banana has been visited by fruit flies, the eggs will soon hatch. If it is warm, they will turn into flies in about ten days.

DAY 10

BIRDS

MOST BIRDS ARE SHY ANIMALS. They have lots of enemies, and are always on the look out for signs of danger. Birdwatching can be a fascinating hobby, but you must be very quiet. A sudden movement or a loud noise will often scare a bird away. You can study birds in the wild, or encourage them to nest in your own garden or backyard.

77 Outdoor birdwatching

If you go birdwatching you must take along two pieces of essential equipment – a pair of binoculars and a notebook. Binoculars allow you to see birds clearly without having to get too close, and with a notebook you can record what you see. Some birdwatchers take along a field guide, which is a book that shows what each bird looks like. When you go birdwatching, see how many different birds you can spot in a day.

You will need:

Pencil   Notebook   Crayons

Use your notebook to sketch what you see

Eyepiece lens

Binoculars should be light and have a good magnification

Keeping notes
You can make notes about the birds you see, or better still, why not draw them and colour them in. A quick drawing is often a good way of remembering an unusual feature, such as the shape of a bird's wing, or the way it flies.

Using binoculars
The best birdwatching binoculars magnify by about eight or ten times. Some binoculars magnify more, but they are heavy and quite difficult to use.

78 Make a bird hide

If you want to spend the whole afternoon birdwatching and study birds more carefully why not make a bird hide. Once inside a hide, you are completely camouflaged. You will be able to have a close look at the daily activities of birds, without them being aware of your presence. In your hide you can use your binoculars and make detailed notes about all the birds you see. You can look at the shape and colour of birds, and watch the way they live. The hide is built just like a tent. You will need an adult to help you.

Adult help is essential

You will need:

4 screws or nails 10 cm (4 in) long   8 poles   Wood glue   Screwdriver

PLUS
8 metal eyes
10 tent pegs
5 guy ropes
Hammer

4 poles (uprights)
1.5 m (5 ft) long
4 poles (cross-bars)
1 m (3 ft) long

Camouflaged netting

1. Hammer a nail to the top of each upright; leave 5 cm (2 in) protruding. Screw the eyes to the ends of the cross-bars and use some glue for extra strength.

3. Tie a guy rope around the top of each upright, make sure that it is 45° to the corner of the frame. Use a tent peg to anchor each guy rope to the ground.

5. Peg down three sides of the netting. Decide on the best side for entry to the hide. Cover the hide with some leaves to complete the camouflage.

Camouflaged netting

2. Lift up the poles and cross-bars so they are upright. Now make sure the frame is standing in a square.

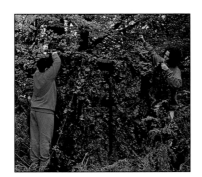

4. Check that each of the guy ropes is tightly anchored to the ground. Throw the camouflage netting over the frame and guy ropes.

6. Once you are inside the hide, clear a hole on each side to give you a good all-round view. You are now ready to do some interesting birdwatching.

Wooden poles

79 Make a nest-box

Finding a home can be a difficult task for a small bird. The nest must not only be sheltered from wind and rain, it must also be beyond the reach of cats and other predators. You can encourage birds to breed in your garden by making a wooden nest box. The finished box is designed to last for many years, but will need cleaning out every autumn after the family of birds has left.

Adult supervision is essential

You will need:

Sandpaper

Screws

Wood

Screwdriver

PLUS Jigsaw, Drill, Plane, Saw, Hinge, Fastening hook

Wood 2 cm (³/₄ in) thick:
A Back panel 25 cm x 15 cm (10 in x 6 in)
B Floor 11 cm x 15 cm (4 ½ in x 6 in)
C Front panel 20 cm x 15 cm (8 in x 6 in)
D Roof 20 cm x 22 cm (8 in x 9 in)
E 2 side panels 15 cm (6 in) wide, rear height 25 cm (10 in), front height 20 cm (8 in)
F Fixing panel 40 cm x 10 cm (16 in x 4 in)

1. Make an entrance hole 29 mm (1¹/₈ in) in diameter in the front panel (C). Sand smooth any rough bits. In the other panels, drill pilot holes for the screws, as shown below left.

2. Plane the top of the back and front panels (A and C) so the roof can lie flat on top of them. Plane the back of the roof (D) so that it fits snugly against the fixing panel (F) when it is shut.

3. First screw the fixing panel (F) to the back panel (A). Next screw on the side panels (E), the floor (B), and the front (C). Finally, attach the roof (D) by the hinge.

4. Fit the hook to the back of the box. Hang the box at least 2 m (6½ ft) above the ground in a shaded place.

80 Examine an old nest

You should never disturb a nest while its owners are still raising a family. But after the breeding season is over, usually by midsummer, the birds will have flown away, and you can safely collect an old nest to see how it is put together. Make sure it is no longer in use – birds sometimes raise more than one family a year. Remember to wash your hands when you have finished the experiment.

Protect the natural world

You will need:

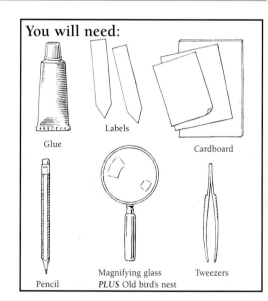

Glue

Labels

Cardboard

Pencil

Magnifying glass

Tweezers

PLUS Old bird's nest

1. Look for an old nest. The most likely place to find one is low down in a hedge or tree. When you have found an empty one, carefully ease it away from its site. You may need to cut through small twigs with secateurs, if the nest has been built around them, in order to release it.

2. Begin your investigation by looking inside the nest. It may still contain food remains and broken shells, giving some clues about the birds who lived in it. You may find types of building material vary according to location.

Small hole keeps out predators

Positioning your nest box
The box is more likely to be used if it is near some leafy branches that can be used as a lookout. But a new owner may not come at once. Birds take time to decide on a new nest.

81 Make an egg-viewing box

This egg viewer works like an X-ray machine, to show you an egg's yolk.

Make hole smaller than egg

1. Cut an oval hole in the lid of the box. Put the torch inside, so that it is shining upwards.

2. Place the egg over the hole so that it is lit from underneath. If the egg is fertilised, a darker patch will be visible; this is the outline of the developing chick.

You will need:

Dark coloured shoebox   Torch

PLUS An egg

This way of looking at eggs is often used to separate fertilised from unfertilised eggs

For the best results use the viewer in a dark room

Different nests may be made of different building materials

Tweezers make it easy to pick up delicate objects

Mud from nest lining

Moss

Broken eggshells

Leaves

3. Using the tweezers, carefully tease apart the nest. Separate the different building materials. Glue a sample of each onto a piece of cardboard and give each one a label.

Nest lining is made of mud

Grass

77

82 Bird food

In autumn, many birds fly off to faraway places, where the weather is warm, and where they can find plenty of food. Other birds stay behind. For these birds food is scarce. Here you will find out how to make some simple bird feeders that will help them survive the harsh winter months. Feeding the birds will also give you a chance to watch them. If you are lucky, the same birds will keep returning.

Adult supervision is advised

Bird pudding is quick to make and is an ideal way to use up your kitchen scraps

You will need:

String

Plastic container or yogurt pot

Bowl

Small saucepan

Wooden spoon

Scissors

Needle

PLUS Kitchen scraps, birdseed, nuts, cooking fat, pine cone, small twig, fresh coconut, and fine mesh bag

Cooking fat

Yogurt pot

Small twig

Leftover cooked vegetables

Porridge oats

Great tit

String

Peanuts in their shells and pecans

Grated cheese

Cooked rice

Mixed nuts

Birdseed

Brown breadcrumbs

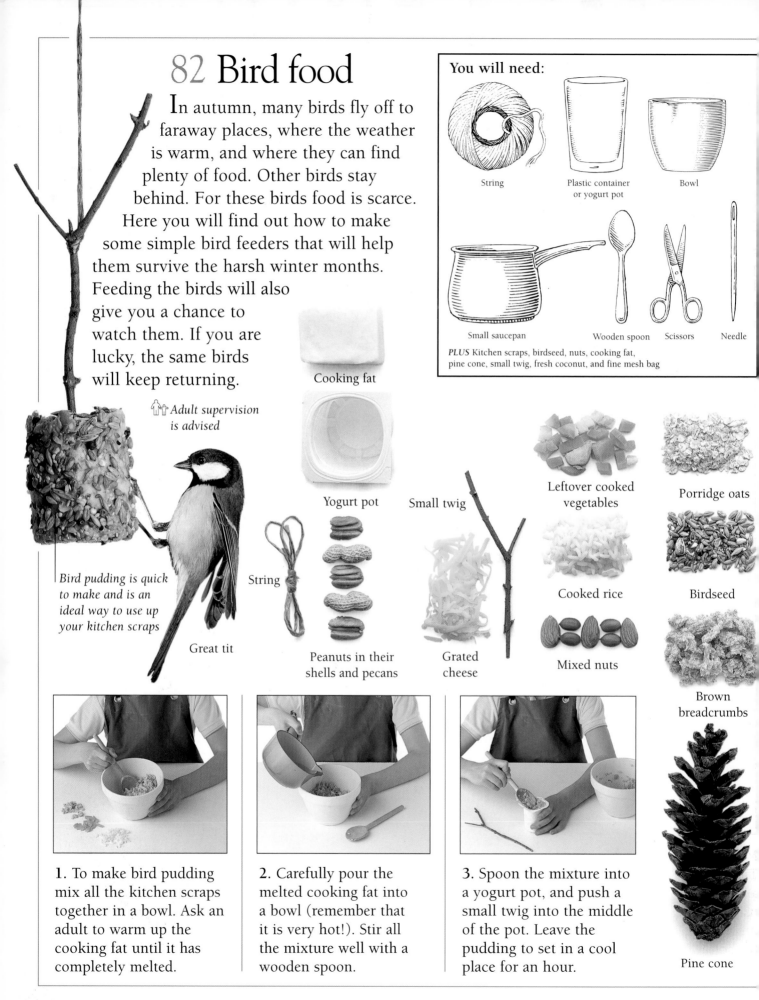

1. To make bird pudding mix all the kitchen scraps together in a bowl. Ask an adult to warm up the cooking fat until it has completely melted.

2. Carefully pour the melted cooking fat into a bowl (remember that it is very hot!). Stir all the mixture well with a wooden spoon.

3. Spoon the mixture into a yogurt pot, and push a small twig into the middle of the pot. Leave the pudding to set in a cool place for an hour.

Pine cone

4. When the pudding has set, squeeze the sides of the pot. Ease the pudding out by pulling the twig. Roll the pudding in birdseed, tie string around the twig.

Make a pine cone perch
Press the pudding mixture between the scales of a pine cone. Tie some string to the pointed end of the pine cone, so you can hang it upside down.

Make a peanut necklace
Tie a knot in the end of a piece of string. Then use a darning needle to push the string through the soft husk that surrounds the nuts.

Fresh coconut is a favourite of many birds

Coconut feeder
Coconuts make an excellent winter food for birds. When the coconut flesh is all eaten, fill the shell with bird pudding.

Pine cone perch
A pine cone gives small birds something to perch on while they are feeding. But birds have to work hard in order to reach all the food.

Bird pudding between the scales

You can watch the birds sway as they feed on the pine cone

Peanuts are an excellent bird food in winter because they are high in fat and protein

Fine mesh bag

Bag of nuts
You can easily make this feeder. Simply add some nuts to a fine mesh bag. Make sure that the bag is beyond the reach of squirrels and other small mammals.

Peanut necklace
Birds quickly learn to peck the husks off peanuts. Never feed the birds with salted nuts, because these can make them sick.

Woodpeckers, tits, and finches can break open the shells

Knot in string

Blue tit

83 Make a feather collection

Throughout their lives, birds gradually shed their feathers and replace them with new ones. This is called moulting, and it helps keep their plumage (body and wing feathers) in peak condition. You can find feathers under trees in parks and other places where birds like to perch. Here you will see how to make special stands to display them.

Adult supervision is advised

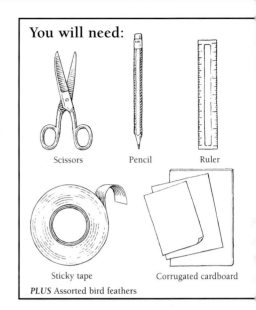

You will need:

Scissors   Pencil   Ruler

Sticky tape   Corrugated cardboard

PLUS Assorted bird feathers

1. If the feathers you find are dusty, clean them in soapy water. When the feathers are dry, pull them through your fingers to arrange them neatly. Spread them on a tabletop and choose your favourite ones to make the collection.

Feather types
A bird's feathers come in many beautiful colours and shapes. They are very light, making it easy for birds to stay in the air.

2. To make the display stands, cut out equal sized strips of corrugated cardboard. Use the sticky tape to fasten the strips together in pairs.

3. Each feather has a stiff central shaft, called a quill. Slide the quill into a hole in the cardboard. This will hold the feather in the stand.

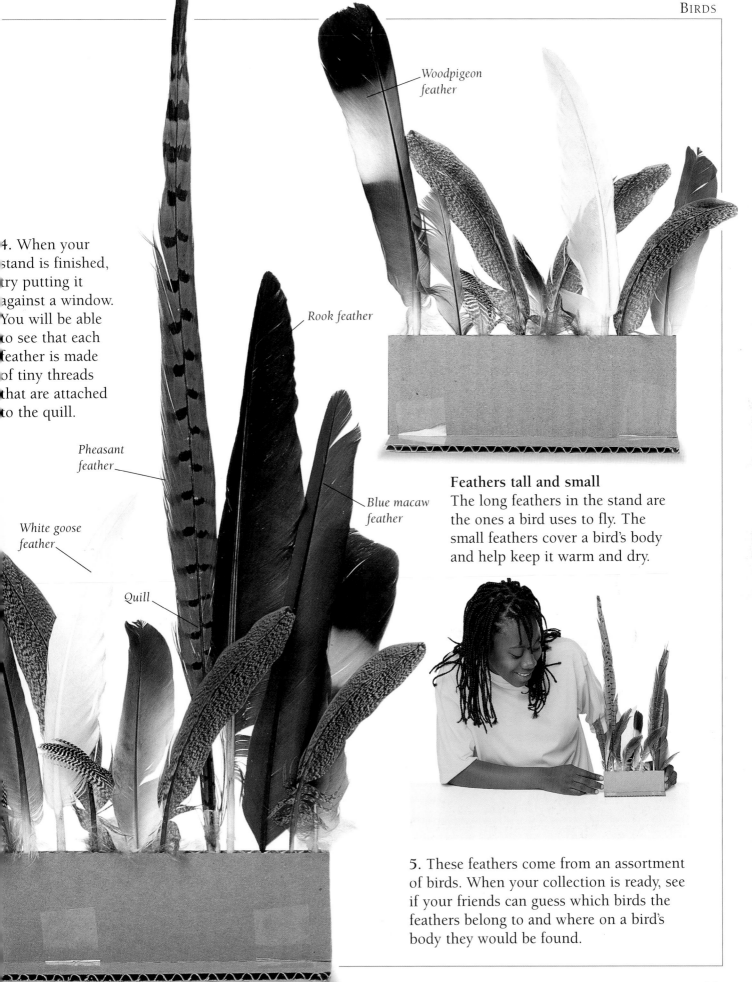

Woodpigeon feather

4. When your stand is finished, try putting it against a window. You will be able to see that each feather is made of tiny threads that are attached to the quill.

Rook feather

Pheasant feather

Blue macaw feather

White goose feather

Quill

Feathers tall and small
The long feathers in the stand are the ones a bird uses to fly. The small feathers cover a bird's body and help keep it warm and dry.

5. These feathers come from an assortment of birds. When your collection is ready, see if your friends can guess which birds the feathers belong to and where on a bird's body they would be found.

81

84 Examine owl pellets

When owls catch small animals, they swallow them whole. Later on, they cough up "pellets", containing the parts they cannot digest. If you look in old barns or under fenceposts, you may be able to find some owl pellets yourself, to discover what an owl has been eating.

Owl pellet is hard and dry

1. Half-fill the glass jar with water and add a few drops of washing-up liquid. Drop in the pellet, screw the lid on tightly, and shake the jar well.

2. Leave the jar to stand for five minutes, and then pour the contents into the sieve. Use the tweezers to pick out skulls, bones, and teeth from the debris.

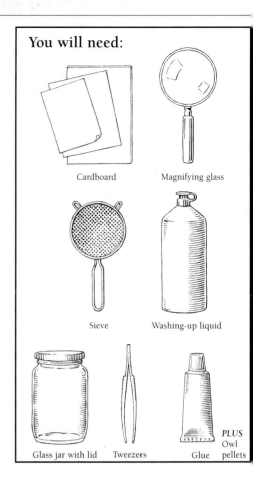

You will need:

Cardboard   Magnifying glass

Sieve   Washing-up liquid

Glass jar with lid   Tweezers   Glue   *PLUS* Owl pellets

85 Design a nature diary

There are so many things to observe in the natural world that it is easy to forget what you have seen. A good way to remember is to keep a nature diary. This kind of diary does not always have to be written in words. You can make drawings of things that you have seen, and you can even include some of the things that you have found. If you keep a diary for a whole year, you can see how plant and animal life changes as one season follows another.

Press some leaves and glue them in your diary

Seedling growing in a jar

You will need:

Glass jar with lid   Coloured card   Pencil   Paintbrush   Paint   Glue

Matted fur

Fur and bones are matted together

Complete pellet

Vole teeth

Shoulder blades

Front limbs   Hip bones

Vole skulls

Leg bones

Jaws

Vertebrae from a starling's backbone

Curved ribs

Incisors

Starling skull

Beak

Wishbone

Ribs

Legs

Claw   Leg bones

Flight feathers

Body feathers

3. Rinse the parts you have collected, and then let them dry. The bones belong to mice, voles, and other small mammals. If you look at the skulls with a magnifying glass, you will be able to see their different shapes. To keep your collection, glue the parts to a piece of cardboard.

Examine the bones with a magnifying glass

Pheasant feathers found in the wood

Draw any new birds that you may see and label any special colours or markings

Polyanthus flower

THE HUMAN BODY

TO MOST PEOPLE, humans and other animals seem very different. Humans are much more intelligent than other animals and can do lots of things that animals can't. Despite all these differences, we are part of the natural world. Just like other animals, we need water, food, and oxygen to survive and we use our senses and our muscles to react to it.

86 Blood flow and gravity

Blood flows through every part of your body, from your head to your toes. It is pushed by your heart, which pumps hard to counteract the pull of gravity. In this experiment you will see what happens if you make your heart work even harder.

Darker hand

Paler hand

Feeling faint
If you get up suddenly, you may sometimes feel slightly dizzy. This happens because your brain runs short of blood until your heart adjusts to your new position.

Blood drains from the hand that is higher up

1. Hold one of your arms up as high as you can, and let the other hang down. Stay like this for at least a minute while the blood travels around them.

Blood collects in the hand that is lower down

2. Compare both hands. You should find that the higher hand is paler than the lower hand. The difference in colour is caused by gravity. It drains blood out of the higher hand, but holds it back in the lower hand.

87 Watch a tooth disintegrate

The strongest substance in your body is tooth enamel. Enamel is very tough, but it cannot cope with chemical attack. See what happens when you put a tooth in a glass of cola. Leave it for 24 hours and then examine it. Cola drinks contain acids. Just like food acids, these chemicals attack teeth and break down their tough outer surfaces.

Cola drinks attack the tooth, causing decay

88 See how fast you grow

As you get older, your body gets bigger and changes shape. But growth is not a smooth process. Newborn babies grow very quickly until they are two years old, then growth slows down. In your early teenage years, growth speeds up again. By the age of 18, most people have reached their adult height.

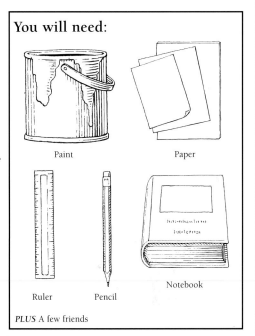
You can see how fast you and your friends are growing by marking your heights on a chart. If you are growing very quickly, you should be able to see the difference in just a few months.

Stand up straight as you are measured

This seven-year-old girl is about three-quarters of her adult height

Your fingers grow faster than your palm

Draw an outline of your hand and see how it changes shape as you grow older

Wear the same shoes to keep your measurements accurate

89 See your pulse rate

Every time your heart beats, it sends a wave of pressure through your blood. This wave is called a pulse. You can feel your pulse with your fingertips on the inside of your wrist where an artery carries blood. The rate of your pulse gives a rough guide to the general health of your heart and body. In this experiment, you will make your pulse visible with the aid of a simple pulse meter made from a piece of putty and a drinking straw.

You will need:
Stop-watch   Plastic putty or modelling clay   Drinking straw

1. Hold out one of your hands with the inside of your wrist facing towards you. Use your fingertips to feel for the pulse in your wrist, below your thumb.

2. Put a blob of putty over the place where you can feel your pulse most strongly. Press a straw into the putty so that it sticks upright from your wrist.

The pulse rate of a ten-year-old is around 80–90 beats per minute

3. Lie the back of your wrist on a table. If the putty is in the right place, the straw will rock slightly every time a pulse passes. You can measure your pulse rate by counting the number of times the straw moves in one minute. Try this first after you have been resting, and then again after taking exercise. How much does your pulse rate change? The rate will be slower after resting and faster after exercise.

90 See your skin change colour

Most people's skin adapts to changing conditions of light. If it is exposed to bright sunshine, it turns darker, which helps to shield it against the harmful rays of the Sun. But what happens if skin is kept in the dark? By covering a small patch of skin with a plaster, you can find out. If the plaster becomes dirty, replace it with a new one on the same patch of skin.

You will need:
Plasters

1. Wrap the sticking plaster around one of your fingers. Leave it on for several days, and expose the rest of your hand to plenty of light during this time.

2. When you are ready, take the plaster off and look underneath. Can you see any difference in the skin colour? Doe the patch of skin feel any different if you touch it?

Skin and moisture
After you have worn a plaster for several days, you may notice that the skin under it has become wrinkly. This happens because skin normally gives off moisture, or sweat. If sweat cannot evaporate, it soaks the outer part of the skin, producing wrinkles.

91 Collect fingerprints

The skin on your fingertips is covered with ridges. These form swirling patterns that are known as fingerprints. With the help of some friends, you can collect different sets of fingerprints, and carry out some detective work to track down a mystery suspect!

Adult supervision is advised

You will need:

Coloured paper   Talcum powder   Magnifying glass   Scissors

Glass   Ruler   Soft pencil   Double-sided sticky tape

Soft brush   Craft knife   Spoon   Pen

1. Mark out ten boxes on a piece of paper. Cut out ten small squares of double-sided sticky tape, and stick a square in each box.

2. On another piece of paper, make a patch of lead powder with the soft pencil. Ask a friend to dab his or her finger on the patch.

3. Peel off the back of the sticky tape, and press the finger on it. Repeat with each finger. Collect sets of prints from other friends.

4. While you are not looking, ask one of your friends to pick up the glass.

5. Scrape off some pencil lead with the knife. Using the back of the spoon, mix the lead with a teaspoon of talcum powder.

Dark paper makes fingerprints easy to see

6. Put one hand inside the glass, and dust the outside with the mixture. The fingerprints should now become visible.

7. Use your fingerprint collection and the magnifying glass to find out which friend picked up the glass. Can you tell which hand they used?

92 Lose your balance

Balance is an ability that most of us take for granted. It tells you which way is up, and also whether you are speeding up, or slowing down. Unlike other senses, balance works by collecting clues from many parts of the body. Follow the four steps here in your bare feet and you will find out what happens when some of those clues are taken away.

You will need:

Blindfold

Cushion

PLUS Large, open space with soft floor

Adult supervision is advised

Outstretched arms adjust your gravity

Sensors on the soles of your feet detect pressure as your body tilts and sways

Be sure an adult is nearby to catch you if you fall

1. Stand on the cushion with your arms held out. The cushion separates your feet from the ground, making it slightly more difficult for you to stand upright.

2. Now stand on one leg. Your brain has only half the information necessary to keep you balanced, and you will start to wobble.

3. Ask an adult to blindfold you. Without clues from your eyes to report the position of your head in relation to its surroundings, your brain has a much harder job telling if you are upright.

4. Now hold your arms by your sides. This makes it even more difficult to stay upright, because moving your arms also helps you to balance. Within a few seconds, you will probably fall over! Try this part of the experiment again, but without the blindfold. Being able to see will help you stay up longer.

Stand on one foot

93 Test your reactions

If you accidentally touch something hot, your hand will pull away before you even have time to think. This is called a reflex, and it is a built-in response that protects you from danger. Reactions are like reflexes, but they have to be learned. The more you use them, the faster they get. See how your reactions improve by testing them on a coloured scale.

Pencil   Glue   Ruler

Scissors   Paper in six different colours, and plain card

Squares of coloured paper

Hold the strip by its upper tip

Coloured scale makes it easy to measure your reactions

1. Cut the coloured paper into equal-sized squares. Glue them to a strip of card, putting the same sequence of colours on both sides.

2. Ask a friend to hold the strip by the upper tip. Place your thumb and forefinger 2.5 cm (1 in) below the strip, ready to catch it as soon as it begins to fall. Ask your friend to drop the card without any warning. Catch it by closing your thumb and forefinger as fast as you can. Where are you holding it?

3. The closer to the bottom you catch the strip, the quicker your reactions. You should be able to improve your time with practice, but may reach a stage (colour) that you cannot get passed.

94 Trick your eyes

Your eyes receive more information than any other sense organ. When you look at anything, your eyes send signals to your brain. Your brain then puts the signals together, and gives you a picture of the outside world. Normally, your eyes and brain give you an exact picture of what you see. But sometimes this does not always happen. Try out these two experiments to reveal your blind spot and see how the brain sometimes misunderstands what it sees.

Blind spot
The experiment below left proves that your eyes actually have a "blind spot". This means that your brain does not always see everything in front of you.

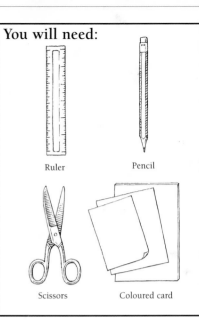

You will need:

Ruler   Pencil

Scissors   Coloured card

1. Take a piece of coloured card and mark a cross and a dot on it. Make sure the dot and cross are at least 10 cm (4 in) apart.

Eye teaser
Draw two lines of the same length and add some arrows as shown. Do both lines look the same length? The lower line looks longer. This is because the direction of the arrows confuses the brain into thinking it is longer, even though it isn't.

Keep your left eye on the cross

2. Hold up the card at arm's length. Make sure that the marked cross is on the right hand side of the card. Cover your right eye and look at the cross with your left eye.

Pull the card slowly away

3. Move the card slowly away, keeping your left eye on the cross. At a certain distance the dot will completely disappear!

95 Test your taste threshold

How strong does the taste of something have to be before you are able to detect that it is there? In this experiment you will be able to discover how good your sense of taste is by testing your ability to taste salt. All you have to do is make up six different strengths of salty water. Sip a little of each mixture, until the taste of salt becomes noticeable.

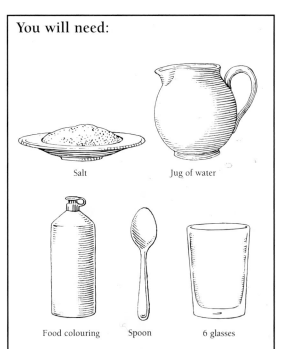

You will need:

Salt

Jug of water

Food colouring

Spoon

6 glasses

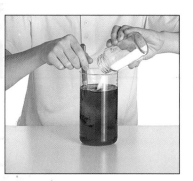

1. Put 25 g of salt into 1 litre of water ($^1/_2$ oz per pint). Add a drop of food colouring to make the dilution visible. Stir it well so that all the salt dissolves.

2. Fill the first glass with the solution. Then pour out some of the solution from the jug until it is only half full. Top it up with water so that the salt solution is halved.

4. Take a sip of the weakest solution to see if you can taste the salt. If not, move to the next glass. As soon as you taste salt, you have reached your threshold level.

Food colouring makes the dilution visible

Strongest solution of salt

3. Put the remaining glasses in a line and fill the second glass with the diluted solution. Repeat step two, so the salt content is again reduced. Keep halving the strength of salty water for each additional glass.

Begin the experiment with the weakest solution of salt

96 Test your blind spot

If you have tried to do the experiment on page 90, you will have discovered that each of your eyes has a small "blind spot". But when you look around, there are no gaps in your vision. This is because our eyes are constantly flicking about, so any gap rarely stays in the same place for long. This experiment proves that even when you focus on an object and keep your eyes quite still, your brain will fill in any gaps by guessing the missing details.

1. Using a compass and a felt-tip pen, draw two circles on a sheet of card. Make the large circle 15 cm (6 in) in diameter and the small circle 2 cm (³/₄ in) in diameter.

2. Place the centre of the protractor on the centre of both circles. Now mark dots at intervals of 15° all the way around the protractor. Do the same on the other side of the circle. When you are finished, you should have 24 dots altogether.

Inside of the circle is blank

Dot here

3. Draw a line connecting each 15° dot to the small circle. Leave the inside of the small circle blank, so you have a pattern like a spoked-wheel. Mark a dot towards the end of the right horizontal spoke, as shown above.

Stare straight at the dot with your left eye

Hold the card at arm's length

Protractor

Compass

4. Keep your right eye covered and look at the dot with your left eye. Move the card backwards and forwards, until the centre circle falls on your blind spot. Instead of vanishing, the centre circle is full of spokes. This is because your brain "fills in" the area that the eye does not see, with an image that it expects to see. In the case of this experiment, it is a spoked-wheel, and not an empty circle.

97 Feel heat

Whenever you sense something, your brain soon adapts to it. Therefore, if you touch something warm, then touch something cool, the cooler object will feel warmer than it really is. Try out this experiment and see if you can fool your temperature receptors.

Adult supervision is advised

You will need:

3 jars

Water
PLUS Food colouring (optional)

1. Fill the jars with cold water, warm water, and hot water (not too hot to touch). Put one finger in the hot water and another finger in the cold water. Leave them for one minute.

Your brain gradually gets used to the two different temperatures

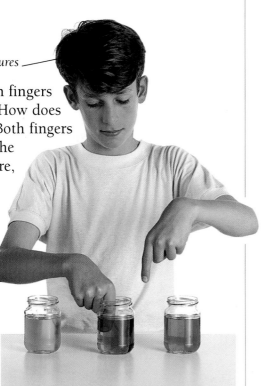

2. Now put both fingers in warm water. How does the water feel? Both fingers are in water of the same temperature, but your brain seems to think otherwise. The temperature feels cooler on one finger and warmer on the other.

98 Test touch

Millions of tiny nerve endings are scattered throughout our skin. With the help of a friend you will discover that different points of your skin are sensitive to different feelings.

You will need:

Ice cubes   2 plastic cups   Hot water   Ruler

Crayon   Metal paperclips   Fine-tipped pen   Pin or needle   Squared paper

1. Draw a grid of small squares on your friend's hand. Now draw four similar grids on squared paper. Heat a paperclip in hot water, cool another in ice.

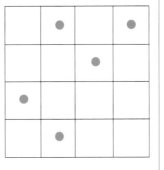

2. Touch each square of skin with a hot paperclip and chart on the grid where your friend can feel the heat of the paperclip.

3. Repeat with the cold paperclip, the crayon, and the pin. On each grid, chart where your friend feels cold, pressure, and discomfort. Examine the four skin maps. You should find that each square of skin tested feels different sensations.

99 Hidden tastes

Some flavours are so strong that they block out other flavours, even when present in small amounts. Here is an experiment that you can try on a friend. See how a strong flavour (salt) can mask a weaker flavour (sugar) by testing a friend's sense of taste. Don't tell your friend what is in each glass. See if he or she can guess that there are actually two substances dissolved in the water.

You will need:

4 glasses of water   Teaspoon

Saucer of salt
Saucer of sugar

1. Stir a teaspoon of salt into each glass of water. Now add half a teaspoon of sugar to the first glass, one to the second, one and a half to the third, and two teaspoons to the fourth.

2. Ask your friend to taste the mixture in each glass, starting with the one that has the least sugar. See if they can tell that the water contains something other than salt.

3. Which mixture makes them realise this? Try the experiment on other friends to see if they taste the sugar in different mixtures. Who has the sharpest taste buds?

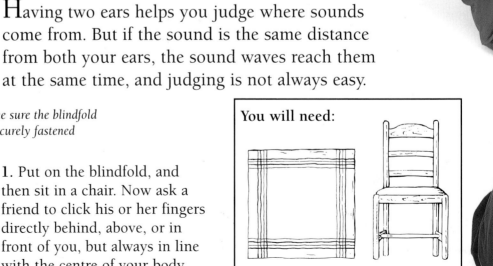

Salt dissolved
in the water

Salt

Sugar

100 Confuse your ears

Having two ears helps you judge where sounds come from. But if the sound is the same distance from both your ears, the sound waves reach them at the same time, and judging is not always easy.

Make sure the blindfold is securely fastened

You will need:

Handkerchief   Chair

1. Put on the blindfold, and then sit in a chair. Now ask a friend to click his or her fingers directly behind, above, or in front of you, but always in line with the centre of your body. Can you tell where the sound is coming from every time?

101 Judge sound direction

Like the experiment on the opposite page, this one shows you how your ears work together. Here, you will find out how good you are at pinpointing sounds which come from many different directions.

You will need:

Blindfold   Chair

1. Put on a blindfold, and then sit on the chair with some of your friends arranged around you in a circle. Ask them to click their fingers at random, so you do not know who is going to make the next click.

It is easier to locate sound in some parts of the circle

2. Each time someone clicks, see if you can point to them. Your friends should then tell you if you are right or wrong.

What happens?
Sound reaches one of your ears before the other. Your brain uses this time difference to locate the sound.

Index

A

air, 6, 7, 23, 30, 31
animal behaviour, 15, 66, 67
animals, 10, 12–15, 17, 19, 24, 25, 29, 33, 46, 50, 54, 60–63, 66, 67, 70, 71, 74, 79, 82–84
  nocturnal, 70, 71
  shelled, 19
  small 62–73, 82
  underground, 22, 23, 26–28
  underwater, 17
  antennae, 69
  aquarium, 15, 60

B

bacteria, 8
balance, 88
bark rubbing, 57
beans, 31, 33, 35, 39
  mung, 48, 49
bee nestbox, 65
bees, 46, 47, 65
beetles, 61
birds 74–83
  feathers, 80, 81, 83
  feeder, 78
  food, 78, 79
  hide, 75
  pudding, 79
  seed, 78, 79
blood, 36, 72, 86
  flow, 84
  pressure, 86
brain, 84, 88, 90, 92, 93, 95
butterflies, 46, 47, 64

C

cacti and succulentss, 42,43
camouflage, 75
caterpillars, 64
  house, 64
cats 70, 76
cells, 6, 7, 10–13
centipedes, 28, 61
chemicals, 16, 30, 35, 51, 53
  attack by, 85
colour, 7, 41, 50–52, 83, 91
  changing, 86
  scale, 89
compost, 9, 30, 38, 39, 42–44, 56
  heap, 9, 67
conifers, 55
cress, 30, 41, 48, 49
cuttings, 40
  runners, 40
  stem, 40

D E

danger signs, 7
decay, 8, 60, 61
disinfectant, 58
dry, 66, 67
drying 51–53, 58, 64
ears, 94, 95
earthworms, 22, 27, 63
egg-viewing box, 77
eggs, 65, 72, 73, 77
ethology, 66, 67
evaporation, 7, 8, 86
eyes, 88, 90, 92

F

feather, 80, 81, 83
  collection of, 80, 81
  plumage, 80
  size, 81
  type, 8
feeding 17, 46, 47, 64, 65
fertilization, 77
fertilizer, 9

fish, 15, 17
flowers, 7, 9, 36, 44–47, 50–54, 83
  artificial, 65
  dissection of, 50
  dried arrangement, 52
  preserving, 53
  pressing, 51
  reproductive organs of, 50
food, 15, 24, 25, 31, 45–47, 54, 60, 61, 66, 67, 72, 76, 78, 79, 84
  for bait, 24, 25
freezing, 34
frost, 34
fruit, 9, 12, 24, 25, 38, 67, 72, 73, 78, 79
  bananas, 9, 72, 73
  pips and pits, 38
fruit flies, 72, 73
fungus, 54, 59

G

gardens, 44–49
  butterfly, 46, 47
  salad, 48, 49
  window 44–47
germination, 31, 33, 36, 37, 39, 49, 56
girdle scar, 54
grass, 29, 30, 77
gravity, 35, 84, 88
growth, 16, 30–33, 36–39, 48, 49, 56

H

hatching, 73
hearing, 94, 95
heart, 84, 86
heat, 54, 58, 73, 93
heathers, 46, 47
herbs, 46, 47
human body, 84–95
humus, 29

I L

insects, 16, 28, 46, 47, 60–62, 68, 69, 72, 73, 82
ladybird, 28
leaf skeleton, 57
leaves, 7, 8, 27–30, 32–40, 44, 54, 56, 57, 62, 64, 71, 82
lettuce, 34, 35
light, 17, 26, 33, 38, 48, 54, 66, 67, 69, 73, 86
litmus paper, 22, 23

M

mammals, small, 83
mice, 83
microscope, 6, 11
migration, 76, 77
minerals, 22, 27, 29, 35, 37
mini-desert, 42, 43, 45
moisture, 66, 67, 86
moth, 69
moth trap, 69
mould, 8, 58, 60
  bread, 58
  growing a, 58
  leaf, 60
moulting, 64, 80
muscles, 84
mushrooms / toadstools, 59

N O P

nature diary, 82, 83
nectar, 46, 47, 65
nerves, 93
nest-box, 76, 77
nests, examining old, 76
nesting site, 65
owl, 82
  pellets, 82, 83
oxygen, 6, 84
pine cone, 60, 61, 78, 79
  perch, 79
pit trap, 24, 25
plants, 9, 11–18, 26, 27, 29–31, 33–37, 39–45, 50, 54, 82, 83
  annual, 34

climbing, 39
deciduous, 34
desert 42, 43
evergreen, 34
flowering, 44–47
leafy, 40
spider, 40
trailing, 44, 46
plaster cast, 71
plaster of paris, 71
pollen, 50
polyanthus, 83
pondwater, 14, 16, 17
protein, 79

Q R

quadrat, 12
rain, 31, 76
recycling, 9
reflex action, 89
rhododendron, 34
rockpool, 17
roots, 7, 32, 33, 35–38, 40, 42, 45, 47, 48

S

sand, 27, 42, 43, 70, 71
sap, 36, 62
seashore, 18
seasons, 45, 46, 62, 64, 65, 72, 76, 78
seedlings, 30, 39, 49
seeds, 30, 31, 34, 37–41, 48–50, 56, 58
senses, 63, 84, 88, 90–95
shells, 14, 18, 19
sight, 90, 92
skin, 86, 87, 93
  map, 93
skulls/skeletons, 82, 83
slugs, 28, 67
snails, 28, 72
soil, 8, 14, 22, 23, 26–30, 35, 37–40, 42–47, 49, 56, 60
  acidic, 22, 23
  alkaline, 22, 23
sound, 15, 94, 95
  direction of, 95
  waves, 94
spiders, 28, 61, 62, 68
  silk, 68
  web, 68
spore print, 59
spores, 58, 59
starch, 35
starling, 83
sugar, 12, 13, 94

T

taste, 91, 94
teeth, 82, 83, 85
tooth decay, 85
  enamel, 85
temperature, 23, 34, 38, 39, 41, 46, 47, 93
thermometer, 23
terrarium, 60, 61
touch, 63, 93
tracks, animal 70–72
  cat, 70
  deer, 71
  snail, 72
  tiger, 70
trees, 8, 36, 38, 54–62, 76, 77, 80
  age of, 55
  deciduous, 54, 55
  evergreen, 54, 55
  height of, 55
tubers, 35
twigs, 54, 64, 71, 76, 79

V W

vegetables, 8, 9, 11, 13, 30, 31, 32, 34–36, 39, 59, 61, 78
  leafy, 34, 61
  root, 32, 35, 36, 39
vitamins, 48
vole, 83
walking on water, 16

water, 6–8, 10, 12–14, 16, 17, 22, 27, 29–33, 35–49, 54, 56–58, 60, 61, 70, 84, 91, 93, 94
  distilled, 22
  filtration, 14, 16
  freshwater, 14
  loss, 8
  seawater, 14
  vapour, 7, 8
weeds, 9, 28
whales, blue 62
wind, 44, 50, 76
wood, 60
woodland, 26, 60, 61
woodlice, 61, 66, 67

Acknowledgements

Dorling Kindersley would like to thank:
The following children for acting as models: Lia Buddle, Alisdair Cairns, Melissa Chu, Alexandra and Nicholas Denton, Leo Dudley, Ashanti Fearon, William Finnegan, Liam Francis, John Gill, Ben and James Highmore, Patora Ho, Sam Jacobson, Camay Jones, Goran Kanlil, Sharon Lucas, Sophia Nawaz, Lika Razaeince, Alex O'Reilly, Tanisha Russell, Samantha Schneider, Sophie Shannon, Amy and Lucy Smith, and Gemma Taylor. Noltan St. Louis for making the compost box, Martin Smith and Julia Harris for supplying additional props, and Year Four at George Tomlinson School in Leytonstone, London.

Additional special photography: Jane Burton, Peter Chadwick, Andy Crawford, Geoff Dann, Mike Dunning, Steve Gorton, Dave King, Stephen Oliver, Tim Ridley, and Kim Taylor.

Illustrations: Jonathan Wolstenholme
Index: Marion Dent
Picture research: Jo Carlill

With special thanks to David Graham for design assistance

Picture credits
(a = above, b = below, c = centre, l = left, r = right, t = top)
Bruce Coleman Limited: 67cra, 70cr
Ron and Christine Foord: 61cr
Frank Lane Picture Agency: 73cl
Harry Smith Collection: 36b

Every effort has been made to trace the copyright holders of photographs, and we apologize for any unavoidable omissions.